U.S. Security Assistance

U.S. Security Assistance

The Political Process

Edited by
Ernest Graves
The Center for Strategic and
International Studies
Georgetown University

Steven A. Hildreth
The Center for Strategic and
International Studies
Georgetown University

Lexington Books
D.C. Heath and Company/Lexington, Massachusetts/Toronto

The views and conclusions expressed in this volume are solely those of the individual authors and do not purport to represent the policies of any government agencies of the United States or of the Georgetown University Center for Strategic and International Studies.

The following newspapers have kindly granted permission to quote from material that originally appeared in their pages. Copyright for each of these quotations resides with the particular newspaper.

Library of Congress Cataloging in Publication Data

Main entry under title:

U.S. Security assistance.

Includes index.
1. Military assistance, American—Addresses, essays, lectures. 2. United States—Military relations—Foreign countries—Addresses, essays, lectures. 3. United States—Foreign relations—1945- —Addresses, essays, lectures. I. Graves, Ernest, Lt. Gen. II. Hildreth, Steven A. III. Title: US Security assistance. IV. Title: United States security assistance.
UA12.U18 1985 355'.032'0973 84-47688
ISBN 0-669-08355-0 (alk. paper)

Published simultaneously in Canada
Printed in the United States of America on acid-free paper
International Standard Book Number: 0-669-08355-0
Library of Congress Catalog Card Number: 84-47688

Contents

Figures and Tables

Figures

Tables

Preface

The idea for the study that led to this book came from a number of people who have had a deep interest in security assistance for many years. They were increasingly concerned about the disagreement over the program and saw a need to understand better why the program is so controversial. There had been extensive study of the program as a policy instrument, but not of attitudes toward security assistance—a major determinant in policy decisions.

This book is the culmination of ten months of study involving a large number of people. Many contributed their views in discussions of perceptions of security assistance and how these influence programmatic decisions. The authors conducted these discussions on a not-for-attribution basis, and it would be inappropriate to mention these contributors by name in this book.

We do wish to express appreciation for the help of several people who made important contributions to the study effort. Dr. Fred Ikle, Under Secretary of Defense for Policy, and Lt. Gen. Philip Gast, Director, Defense Security Assistance Agency, showed a keen interest in the study and were active participants in the meetings to discuss study results. Dr. Amos Jordan, President of the Center for Strategic and International Studies, Georgetown University, gave constant leadership and encouragement as project supervisor and moderator of the study seminars. Dr. James Schlesinger, CSIS Senior Adviser, served on the steering committee for the study and was the keynote speaker for the seminar series to present and receive the comments of senior administration officials and members of Congress on the study results. Dr. Henry Gaffney, Director of Plans, DSAA, and Mark Shwartz of the DSAA Plans Directorate gave invaluable advice in their capacity as DOD project advisers. Colonel Richard Lalley, Dr. Andrew Semmel, Helen Moore, and Judith Frey of DSAA provided important data for our analyses. Christine Viezens, CSIS research assistant, made a number of substantive contributions to the study, particularly the portion covered in chapter 2. David Wallace, CSIS research assistant, and Michael Hayes,

Georgetown University work-study intern, also made important contributions to the project. Mary Park, CSIS conference coordinator, arranged the congressional seminar series. Charlene Harding typed much of the manuscript.

While the authors owe much to the help received from all who participated, they are solely responsible for the conclusions reached, and no inference of endorsement by others should be drawn.

We hope that this book will contribute to the dialogue on security assistance and help, at least in a small way, in informing a larger public and in the development and implementation of policy.

Introduction

James R. Schlesinger

The American attitude toward security assistance remains rather paradoxical. For over thirty-five years that program has been one of this nation's principal—and most effective—instruments of foreign policy and defense. Yet it enjoys little public support and is regularly the object of criticism and controversy. What are the nature of this national ambivalence, the reasons for it, and the implications for the future of security assistance as a policy tool?

To answer these questions the Center for Strategic and International Studies of Georgetown University undertook a study of the perceptions regarding security assistance and their effect on the program. Better understanding of such matters, it was believed, might well lead to wiser decisions, a greater degree of consensus and, thus, the more effective use of security assistance in protecting U.S. interests around the world.

The study confirmed what should be apparent: the highly political character of the program. Various groups with sharply competing objectives are constantly striving to influence government policy. Because both the execution and the effects of security assistance are rather distant from the direct experience of either the public or the Congress, influence may be gained by the shaping—that is, the manipulation—of perceptions. In politics, after all, perception is frequently more important than substance. One might go a step further and argue that in this area perceptions are the main substance—"the reality"—of the politics of security assistance. In this book the aim was not so much to contrast perception and substance, but rather to appraise how perceptions influence the substance and the success of the program.

The study relied on two research tools: first, review and analysis of the literature, the public record, media reporting, and executive branch and congressional documents, and second, discussions with senior officials of the executive branch, members of Congress, executive and congressional staff members, and representatives of interest groups.

The five chapters of this book cover five major areas of investigation. The first chapter focuses on the relation between major international developments over the last thirty-five years and changes in the security assistance program during that period. The second chapter sifts through the vast array of views on the program expressed by the executive branch, the Congress, and the media during the annual deliberations on the budget. The third chapter examines the attitudes of decision makers in the executive branch and the Congress through a series of private interviews. The fourth chapter appraises the views and the influence exerted by the public and the interest groups. The final chapter relates the views of the participants to the decisions reached about the program—and suggests how a better understanding of this relationship can be used to improve security assistance as an instrument of U.S. policy.

The book reminds us that there is no panacea for what ails the world or neat prescriptions for U.S. international involvement. Like the ills they seek to address, decisions on U.S. foreign policy and supporting security assistance are complex. The chapters that follow examine this complexity and offer insights, but they also challenge the reader to weigh the evidence and reach conclusions of his own.

Thoughtful students of U.S. foreign and defense policy will find that this book deepens their understanding of congressional–executive relations, as each branch seeks to exert its influence over the conduct of America's external affairs. Neither the political dynamics of the security assistance program nor how the executive–legislative rivalry has played out since the program's inception are widely understood. This book addresses such issues forthrightly. It is gratifying therefore to see these results made available to a wider audience.

1
The Role of Security Assistance in Historical Perspective

Richard F. Grimmett

Introduction

Too often security assistance is discussed in isolation rather than in relation to the national goals and the world environment that are the basis for the program. This opening chapter reviews the evolution of the U.S. security assistance program to afford an understanding of the historical and geopolitical context in which decisions about the program are made.

The overall goal of U.S. defense and foreign policy since World War II has been to foster a stable, peaceful world conducive to national security, economic prosperity, and individual freedom. It has been determined that the United States has vital overseas interests and that protecting those interests depends upon association with other nations sharing our basic aims. This goal, however ambitious and at times elusive, has been at the center of U.S. security policy planning. The principal international problems confronting the United States have been increasing political instability in the developing world, the ever-present threat of Soviet support of political and military adventurism, and the threat inherent in the overall growth of Soviet military power.

Domestically, the pursuit of international stability and peace involves problems faced by all free and democratic societies. These include, most notably, divergent views on the best approach to foreign and defense policy and the competition for funds between the needs of domestic programs and the requirements of foreign military and economic programs overseas. Closed societies do not have to answer their people directly on such questions. The leadership of

---

U.S. data in this chapter are provided by fiscal year and, unless otherwise indicated, are expressed in current dollars.

totalitarian and authoritarian states imposes its will and commits the resources it feels are necessary to achieve a given foreign policy end. The United States attempts to strike a balance between domestic and foreign requirements through judgments made by its elected executive and legislative representatives. These judgments have been made more difficult by the growing complexity of the international system and the diffusion of economic and military power.

The judgments reached as to what assets should be committed to support U.S. national interests overseas are reflected in the data set forth in this chapter. As these data indicate, allocation of specific security assistance program resources has changed over time in response to international events in an effort to utilize these programs to support U.S. foreign policy objectives.

Since the inception of the program just after World War II, U.S. policymakers have viewed security assistance as an important and flexible instrument for the pursuit of U.S. foreign and defense policy objectives. It has been used to help friendly and allied nations acquire and maintain the capability to defend themselves, serving both specific U.S. national interests and the collective security of the free world. It has been used to demonstrate tangible U.S. support for nations whose defense was deemed vital to U.S. security. Security assistance has also been used to supplement economic aid when U.S. policymakers judged that a country lacked the means to provide for its own defense, or that diversion of its resources from economic development to defense spending would prove counterproductive. It has also been employed in conjunction with a commitment to use U.S. military power if need be to deter regional conflict or to keep such conflict at the lowest possible level when it occurred.

This chapter relates the beginning and evolution of the U.S. security assistance program to the major international developments of the last thirty-five years. It describes how the government has responded with grants of military equipment and training under the Military Assistance Program (MAP), the International Military Education and Training (IMET) program, and with Foreign Military Sales (FMS), both cash and credit, to help friendly states deal with security problems judged important to the United States. Data are presented, as well, to show the trend in the size of these programs in relation to other major elements of the federal budget.

Evolution of the Collective Security Concept

To understand the role played by the security assistance program in U.S. foreign policy, it is necessary to examine the origins of the concept of collective security in the period immediately after World War II and the relationship of that concept to security assistance. Once the concept of collective security was firmly rooted, security assistance became a key element in its implementation.

The concept of collective security in the post-World War II period had its origins in the shattered hopes for a lasting reconciliation between the Communist and non-Communist worlds. It also stemmed from the "lessons" learned from World Wars I and II that "preemptive" alliances could deter conflict and that to refrain from entering into alliances until conflict had begun increased the risk of war. The United Nations had not fulfilled the expectations of its founders to serve as a major bulwark of international order. The Soviet Union began to exploit the economic and political dislocation in Europe and Asia caused by the war to advance its own foreign policy ends, which were clearly at variance with those of the United States.

The first phase in the Soviet Union's expansion of its power in Eastern Europe was the consolidation of its effective authority in such countries as Bulgaria, Romania, Poland, and Hungary. With Soviet troops already in these countries it was easy to create puppet governments subservient to Moscow. The "democratic" governments envisioned by the Yalta agreements became satellites of the Soviets through subversion of the electoral process and the intimidating presence of Soviet military power.

In 1946 and 1947 the Soviet Union attempted to press its interests in the Mediterranean and Near East through a series of threatening actions. In early 1946 the USSR initially refused to withdraw its troops from Iran, hoping to maintain a presence in that strategically located state. The strong response of the United States and Great Britain indicated that they were prepared to use force to protect Iran and led the Soviets to withdraw their forces.

In August 1946 the Soviets demanded that Turkey revise the 1936 Montreux Convention governing passage through the Turkish straits into the Aegean from the Black Sea. Acquiescence to this demand would have given the Russians domination over Turkey as well as administrative control of the Turkish straits. The United States responded to this Soviet demand by sending a naval task force to the Mediterranean. Two weeks later the United States rejected the Soviet demand. In the face of this firm opposition, the Soviets backed off from their initiative.

In February 1947 the British informed the United States that they could no longer be responsible for the burden of protecting Greece from ongoing Communist guerrilla attacks or for general military and economic support of either Greece or Turkey. At the time Greece was in serious difficulty and on the verge of economic and military collapse. It seemed evident that should Greece fall to Communist subversion, the position of the free world throughout the Mediterranean, Near East, and Europe would be gravely threatened.

The response of U.S. policymakers to this cumulative evidence of Soviet expansionist intentions was to seize the immediate crisis in Greece to launch bold new policy initiatives. The aim of these initiatives was to restore political and economic stability to key regions of the world, especially Europe, which could halt the potential for Soviet domination of them. The first of these initiatives was President Harry Truman's request for $400 million for a program of military and economic assistance for Greece and Turkey.

The Truman Doctrine and Containment

In his address before Congress on March 12, 1947, making his aid request for Greece and Turkey, President Truman stated his belief that "it must be the policy of the United States to support free peoples who are resisting attempted subjugation by armed minorities or by outside pressures." President Truman argued that if the United States failed to support the cause of the free peoples of the world, it would very likely endanger world peace and the welfare of the United States.

The president's speech became the cornerstone of what came to be known as the Truman Doctrine. It also was the beginning of a policy of active "containment" of the Soviet Union. In its broadest sense this policy envisaged resistance to the expansion of Soviet influence and power, using whatever means were necessary whenever such an expansion threatened to undermine the independence of non-Communist nations of the world, either through direct aggression or internal subversion. In practice, the policy of containment led to the establishment of several U.S. security assistance programs and, ultimately, to a series of mutual defense pacts to give it force and effect as the perception of direct Soviet military threats to the West increased.

Marshall Plan

Immediately following congressional passage of the Greek–Turkish aid program in May 1947, the Truman administration began efforts to provide massive economic assistance to much of war-torn Europe. Secretary of State George C. Marshall set forth the plan during a speech at Harvard University on June 5, 1947. He outlined the aid program as an effort to revive the global economy "so as to permit the emergence of political and social conditions in which free institutions can exist."

The economic impact of World War II on Europe was profound. Industrial centers had been destroyed, unemployment was high, and general living standards had been reduced notably, making Europe vulnerable to Communist subversion and infiltration. U.S. policymakers saw the rejuvenation of Europe's economy as vital to U.S. national security interests. Although the concept of direct economic assistance to foreign governments had been historically unpopular in the United States, these circumstances posed such a clear threat to U.S. security interests that Truman administration officials and their allies in Congress argued that a departure from previous practices was warranted.

The Marshall Plan was introduced in Congress as the Economic Cooperation Act (ECA). Its overwhelming approval in March 1948 was hastened by the Communist coup in Czechoslovakia in late February, which served to illustrate the vulnerability of Europe. By adopting the Marshall Plan, the United States committed itself to supplying billions of dollars to recipients in Western Europe to help them bring about economic recovery.

Creation of NATO

The Truman administration soon concluded that economic assistance by itself would not be sufficient to forestall Soviet expansionism in Europe if European nations did not also have a credible military capability to resist it. Thus, in March 1948, with the United States's encouragement, the United Kingdom, France, and the Benelux countries signed a treaty of collective security that came to be known as the Brussels Pact.

A Senate resolution approving U.S. association with such "regional and other collective arrangements" and supporting their development for "individual and collective self defense" purposes was introduced by Senator Arthur H. Vandenberg, chairman of the Senate Committee on Foreign Relations, in the spring of 1948. This resolution was unanimously agreed to by the Committee on May 19, 1948, and passed the Senate on June 11, by a vote of 64 to 6. The Vandenberg Resolution played a key role in the developing U.S. commitment to participate in a European collective defense system and it was the basis for U.S. association with Europe in the establishment of the North Atlantic Treaty Organization (NATO) in 1949.

An important impetus for closer association between Europe and the United States in defense was the Soviet blockade of Berlin that began in June 1948. In an effort to force Western occupying powers out of the divided German capital, the Soviets imposed a ban against surface traffic between West Germany (occupied by the United States, France, and the United Kingdom) and the western zones of Berlin located in Soviet-occupied East Germany. In response to this challenge, the United States organized a massive airlift to provide necessary supplies to the citizens of West Berlin. The airlift was an overwhelming success, and after a year the Soviets ended the land blockade. The episode served, however, to highlight continued Soviet willingness to exploit any potential European or Western weakness and provided a powerful argument for stronger efforts in the West to contain Soviet power.

It was in this context that the final action to break the long-standing tradition in the United States of avoiding "entangling alliances" with foreign powers—especially European—took place. On April 4, 1949, the United States and eleven other European nations signed the North Atlantic Treaty, establishing NATO. The creation of NATO was a turning point in post-World War II diplomatic history, demonstrating that the United States had accepted the role of an active agent for the preservation of political and military stability in the world wherever its vital national interests were placed at risk. Through the North Atlantic Treaty, ratified by a Senate vote of 83–13 on July 21, 1949, the United States and twelve other nations committed themselves to consider an "armed attack against one or more of them . . . an attack against them all." The parties agreed that in such an event they would collectively aid the nation or nations attacked through such action as each of the parties deemed necessary, "including the use of armed force."

In 1949 the establishment of NATO with the United States as the leading member was to U.S. policymakers a logical extension of the effort to contain Soviet expansionism and reinforce the economic restoration of the European allies—the aim of the Marshall Plan. A parallel initiative was the U.S. decision to provide strength to the new collective defense system through a major program of military assistance. This program was created through the passage of the Mutual Defense Assistance Act (MDAA) of 1949, in the fall of that year.

Military Assistance Program

To policymakers in the Truman administration, the Military Assistance Program was a necessary element to give credibility to the new NATO alliance. Its intent was to add military capability where it was lacking as an adjunct to the economic assistance program that aimed at stimulating European recovery. Its final approval by Congress was facilitated by President Truman's announcement in late September 1949 that the Soviet Union had exploded an atomic device, thus ending the American monopoly in the nuclear weapons sphere.

The Mutual Defense Assistance Act of 1949 was significant for two reasons. First, it gave the United States authority to provide substantial military assistance to NATO countries, as well as Greece, Turkey, Iran, Korea, and the Philippines. Second, it established the legal basis for the major security assistance program elements that exist to this day. The Military Assistance Program (MAP), which stemmed from the MDAA of 1949, provided for the loan or outright grant of military equipment, materials, and services to eligible nations. In practice, nearly all MAP items were provided on a grant basis. Training was part of the basic MAP program until 1976, when the International Military Education and Training (IMET) program was established as an independent security assistance component. The Foreign Military Sales (FMS) cash and credit program also had its origins in the MDAA of 1949. Through section 408 (e) of the MDAA, the president was permitted to "provide procurement assistance without cost to the United States" to countries seeking U.S. military equipment or associated services or to "enter into contracts for the procurement for transfer" of such materials, equipment, or services to eligible nations.

The scope and nature of the grant MAP, grant training, and FMS cash and credit programs changed significantly from 1949 to the present. Legislative amendments to the MDAA enacted in the mid-1950s and in the 1960s gave greater flexibility in providing credits to eligible nations. Reductions in the levels of the grant MAP program subsequently occurred, especially as industrial nations became increasingly able to pay for U.S. military equipment.

Major security assistance programs and authorities were consolidated in 1951 by the Mutual Security Act in order to place responsibility for implementing the various programs in the hands of a centralized agency. The Mutual Security Acts of 1951 to 1960 authorized funding for foreign military and economic aid programs, which were further consolidated in the Foreign Assistance Act of 1961. The growth of the FMS cash and credit program led to passage of the Foreign Military Sales Act of 1968 to provide separate authorities for that program. The International Security Assistance and Arms Export Control Act of 1976 created the Arms Export Control Act (AECA), which made a wholesale revision of arms export law. It is the AECA, as amended, which governs the FMS cash and credit program today. (See appendix A for an outline of benchmark security assistance legislation.)

Korea and Collective Security in Asia

While the collective security system was being established in Europe, additional challenges confronted the United States in Asia. In late 1949, the fall of China to Mao Tse-tung's Communist forces and the flight of Chiang Kai-shek's Nationalist forces to Taiwan raised concerns among U.S. policymakers about the security of other non-Communist states in the region. These concerns were greatly intensified after the invasion of South Korea in June 1950 by forces from Communist North Korea. The ensuing Korean War, in which the United States played the major combat role, helped consolidate U.S. commitment to support programs that fostered collective security not only in Europe but in Asia as well.

The Korean War raised concerns among U.S. policymakers because it was a direct military challenge by Communist forces to the position of the United States in Asia. Should South Korea fall, Japan would be directly exposed to threats from the Soviet Union and its North Korean ally. The security of the Philippines, Taiwan, and other U.S. friends and allies and Southeast Asia and the Pacific would also be placed in jeopardy. The basic credibility of the United States commitment to act to contain Soviet or other Communist expansionism would be called into question, possibly encouraging Soviet or Communist adventurism elsewhere. Thus, the U.S. war effort in Korea and its expansion of security assistance programs in Asia can best be understood if viewed in this context.

There had been policy disputes within the U.S. government regarding the proper levels of funding for foreign assistance and the appropriate regional emphasis of such aid, since the beginning of the containment policy. There was a general consensus that a serious challenge confronted the United States and the free world in Soviet and other Communist expansionism. In the period from 1947 to 1950, the principal program orientation was European. For it was in that region that the threat to U.S. security interests was seen to be most immediate and to have the gravest potential consequences. The Korean War led to a modification of that emphasis to some degree, if only because of the resources that had to be committed to Asia to carry out wartime operations in Korea. European aid programs continued despite the outbreak of the Korean War, but that war led to a further emphasis for some time on assistance programs aimed at building up defensive capabilities of friendly states in Asia.

By the mid- to late-1950s, security assistance programs that originated in policies designed to confront a Soviet threat in Europe had become much more global in nature. Among the notable extensions of the collective security concept during the early 1950s was the creation of bilateral and multilateral mutual security treaties between Asian nations and the United States. These treaties included the U.S.–Japanese Treaty of 1951, the U.S.–Philippines Treaty of 1951, the ANZUS Pact of 1951 between Australia, New Zealand, and the United States, and the U.S.–Republic of Korea Treaty of 1953.

The establishment of these mutual security treaties with friendly states in Asia served the same U.S. foreign policy purposes in that region as NATO did in Europe. First, the treaties provided a tangible symbol of U.S. support for its respective partners in each treaty arrangement. Second, they provided a basis for U.S. access to important military facilities in strategic locations. These military bases added credibility to the U.S. military deterrent and made possible power projection in the defense of U.S. interests and those of host nations. Third, the treaties provided a basis for developing closer military and political cooperation between the United States and the various cosignatories. In this fashion the concept of collective security was extended and enhanced globally.

The individual Asian and Pacific treaty arrangements reflected the importance that the United States placed on its partners during this period. Japan was seen as a vital linchpin in the Far East, particularly after the Korean war broke out in 1950. Efforts were undertaken to conclude a peace treaty and a security pact with the Japanese soon after the war began. In September 1951 a treaty of peace with Japan and a bilateral mutual security treaty between Japan and the United States were signed—cementing the U.S. commitment to Japan's defense.

Related security treaties between the United States and the Philippines and the United States and Australia and New Zealand (the ANZUS Pact) were also signed in the late summer of 1951. The first treaty provided the basis for continued U.S. access to key military bases in the Philippines and a means of furthering military and political ties for mutual defense. The treaty with Australia and New Zealand provided for similar defense cooperation with these two Pacific democracies. These Asia and Pacific treaties were ratified by the United States Senate on March 20, 1952, and had entered into force by late August 1952.

These treaties provided the collective security framework called for by the major legislative vehicles of the security assistance program during its early years. The Mutual Defense Assistance Act of 1949 declared that U.S. efforts to promote peace and stability required support measures based on the principle of "continuous and effective self-help and mutual aid." Such measures included the furnishing of military assistance essential to enable the United States and other nations "to participate effectively in arrangements for individual and collective self-defense." The MDAA of 1949 directed the president, prior to furnishing assistance under the act, to conclude agreements with eligible nations that in his judgment were necessary to safeguard the interests of the United States and to accomplish the purposes and policies of the act.

The Mutual Security Act of 1951 declared as its purpose the maintenance of the security and promotion of the foreign policy of the United States through the provision of military, technical, and economic assistance to friendly countries. The intent in providing such assistance was to strengthen the mutual security and individual and collective defenses of the free world, to enable friendly nations to develop their resources in the interest of their security and the national interest of the United States, and to facilitate the effective participation of these nations in the collective security system.

Thus was established the clear linkage between the creation of collective security treaties and agreements and the U.S. security assistance program. Assistance from the United States would flow to those nations deemed vital to U.S. security and with whom the United States had concluded mutual defense agreements or arrangements. The levels of U.S. aid discussed below are, not surprisingly, highest for nations with whom we had formal security agreements.

At the end of the Korean War in 1953, the United States also concluded a bilateral mutual security pact with South Korea. This treaty was a logical extension of the U.S. commitment to Korean defense and a further statement of the willingness of the United States to use force in the area to protect its interests and those of its friends.

These security treaty obligations enjoyed general bipartisan support in the 1950s, and the transition from the Truman to the Eisenhower administration in 1953 did not diminish the primary commitment to enhancing the strength of Europe and the North Atlantic Treaty Organization. Although the Korean War was not a popular conflict in the United States, successive crises in Asia led the Eisenhower administration to take steps to strengthen the position of the free nations there through additional treaty commitments. These specific treaties were the Southeast Asia Treaty creating SEATO, signed in September 1954, and the Republic of China Treaty, signed in December of 1954.

Indochina and SEATO

The successes of the Communist Viet Minh forces under Ho Chi Minh in the summer of 1954 led to an agreement that divided Vietnam into two entities, with the Communists controlling the area north of the seventeenth parallel. The collapse of the French in Indochina raised serious concerns in Washington and led to U.S. support for a Western-oriented government in South Vietnam. Thus began the initial commitment that was to grow in the 1960s into a more costly and deep commitment of resources in Southeast Asia.

The concerns for the stability of friendly states in the Southeast Asian region in the wake of the French war in Indochina led the United States to sponsor the Southeast Asia Treaty of September 1954 that created SEATO. The United States, France, Great Britain, the Philippines, Australia, New Zealand, Pakistan, and Thailand joined in this treaty, which provided the basis for a U.S. security guarantee for most of Southeast Asia and the nearby South Pacific areas. In a protocol, the treaty also extended the security mantle to South Vietnam, Cambodia, and Laos. Although the Southeast Asia Treaty was a mutual security arrangement, its structure and language made clear that it was, in practical terms, a vehicle for the unilateral intervention by the United States should it feel its interests in the area were threatened by Communist aggression or subversion.

In a similar fashion, the United States responded in late 1954 to Chinese Communist attacks against two islands controlled by the Nationalists, Quemoy and Matsu, by concluding a bilateral security treaty with Taiwan. To further emphasize the U.S. commitment to maintaining the status quo in the Formosa Strait and contain any attack by the People's Republic of China against Taiwan itself, President Dwight Eisenhower asked Congress in January 1955 for authority to use U.S. military forces to protect Taiwan and nearby territories as he deemed necessary. Congress approved this request through passage of a joint resolution in late January. Thus, by the end of President Eisenhower's first term, the collective security structure that had begun under President Truman with NATO had been extended to most of Asia. The programs of security assistance to support this structure had become an integral part of American foreign policy.

Suez, the Eisenhower Doctrine, and CENTO

Beyond Southeast Asia, there continued to be developments which were to have a bearing on the direction of the U.S. security assistance programs. In 1956 the Suez crisis led to a major diplomatic conflict involving the United States, the United Kingdom, France, and Israel. By opposing the military action of these states against Egypt, the United States brought about the collapse of their Suez campaign and shored up the image of Egypt's President Gamal Abdel Nasser as the leader of Arab nationalism. The resolution of the Suez crisis also marked the beginning of active Soviet involvement in Egypt and other parts of the Arab world, capitalizing on the Arab–Israeli dispute.

In response, in early 1957 President Eisenhower received, through a joint resolution of Congress, authorization to extend American military and economic assistance to the Middle East to combat Communist-inspired armed aggression should any country there request it. In addition, President Eisenhower obtained language in the resolution permitting deployment of American military forces in the region to seek the same end. The Eisenhower Doctrine thus set forth was a further indication of the support that existed in the United States for confronting Soviet challenges that threatened to undermine the stability or security of independent nations in areas considered vital to U.S. national interests.

In the wake of the Suez crisis of 1956 President Nasser of Egypt increased his efforts to promote Pan-Arab nationalism and reduce Western influence in the Middle East. With the support of the Soviet Union, Nasser placed pressure on Jordan, Lebanon, and Iraq in an effort to draw them out of the Western sphere of influence. In the spring of 1957, the United States responded to a Jordanian call for help under the Eisenhower Doctrine by providing military aid and sending a Sixth Fleet task force to the eastern Mediterranean as a show of support for Jordan's King Hussein. This effort materially aided Hussein's effort to stave off an attempt to overthrow him.

In 1958 after the pro-Western government in Iraq was overthrown and the new government joined an alliance with Egypt, U.S. policymakers came to believe that direct intervention in the area might be required to preserve the position of the West. When a civil war broke out in Lebanon in 1958 the United States swiftly sent 14,000 U.S. marines to restore order after a request for assistance from the pro-Western government. As a result of this action, pressures on Lebanon and Jordan by Egypt abated, and the U.S. resolve to act was demonstrated. The lack of an effective counteraction by the Soviets in support of Egypt undermined both Nasser's status in the region and that of the Soviets as a reliable ally.

These events in the Middle East led to closer American association with friendly states in that region. In July 1958 the United States, through an executive agreement, formally adhered to the newly created Central Treaty Organization (CENTO), whose members included the United Kingdom, Iran, Pakistan, and Turkey. The treaty group announced their intent to maintain their collective security and to resist direct or indirect aggression. The United States pledged at the time to give force to its commitment by increasing military aid for Pakistan, Iran, and Turkey.

Through its association with CENTO, the United States completed a formal collective security network that had been developing since the creation of NATO. It also recommitted itself to provide security assistance to nations that had been viewed since the beginning of the MAP program as key bulwarks against the spread of Communist influence in the strategic Middle East, Persian Gulf, and Southwest Asian area. Concern for maintaining access to Persian Gulf oil had been a key element of U.S. policy since the Cold War began, and indeed since World War II. Security assistance to nations that bordered on the Gulf, that were anti-Communist, and that were major oil suppliers to the industrial West was seen as a minimum investment in preserving the long-term security not only of the United States but of its major allies in Europe as well.

When the Kennedy administration entered office in 1961, it inherited the basic Cold War consensus, developed since the late 1940s, that the Soviets and Communist subversion were the main threats to international stability and that security assistance programs had a proper role in supporting U.S. policy interests and peace throughout the world. The geographic distribution and program emphasis of security assistance changed under the Kennedy and Johnson administrations, but these modifications were based as much on the general success of the earlier programs in achieving their goals as on a sense that the programs needed reshaping because of changes in the international political and military environment.

By the early 1960s the security assistance program had achieved notable successes in support of U.S. national security goals. Europe had recovered from the devastation of World War II. The North Atlantic Treaty Organization, the Military Assistance Program, and the Greek and Turkish aid programs had deterred the Soviets on the European continent. NATO members had successfully rebuilt viable military establishments. In Asia, the attempt to overthrow the South Korean government had failed after strong resistance from the United

States in the Korean War effort. As a result of these successes, the high levels of funding for security assistance declined after the Korean War ended. Security program emphasis after the height of the Cold War period shifted to Third World nations that were less industrialized and consequently did not require expensive military hardware from the United States to equip and train their military services. In addition, increasing emphasis was placed in the early and mid-1960s on developmental and economic assistance to combat Communist subversion in the Third World at the expense of funding for purely military oriented security assistance.

Distribution of Security Assistance, 1950–1963

A review of the levels of security assistance program support, FY 1950–FY 1963—the peak Cold War period—will help illustrate how the events discussed above compare with actual levels of assistance provided during this period (see tables 1–1 through 1–5 and table 1–6). It is not surprising to find that Europe and Canada, with a regional level in excess of $18.4 billion, received by far the greatest proportion of grant MAP and grant training program funds during this period. Given American policymakers' emphasis on building up this region after World War II, it is also not surprising to find that this region led in FMS program purchases at a level of over $2.9 billion. West Germany, Canada, and France were the leading purchasers. The top-ranking MAP program and training recipients within this region were France, Italy, and Turkey—all members of NATO.

These funding and support levels show the centrality of Europe in United States strategic planning. In a very real sense the security assistance program was a European-oriented program for most of the period from 1947 to 1963. Although there were policy disputes within the United States government during these years over how to best meet the Soviet military challenge, most agreed that the loss of Europe to Soviet domination would place U.S. security in grave peril. Thus, high aid levels to France, Italy, Turkey, and Greece, and arms sales to West Germany merely reflect a policy decision to provide necessary assets where vital U.S. interests were at stake.

The East Asia and Pacific region ranked second in the share of MAP program and grant training that it received during this time—more than $8.9 billion. The key country MAP recipients were Taiwan, South Korea, South Vietnam, and Japan, in that order. Again, the distribution of these program funds is consistent with American

Table 1–1
Leading Program Participants by Region: Europe and Canada[a]
(thousands of current U.S. dollars)

MAP Program[b]		*FMS (sales) Program Agreements*	
		Fiscal Years 1950–1963	
France	4,442,287	West Germany	1,680,690
Italy	2,492,333	Canada	592,119
Turkey	2,288,034	France	254,590
Greece	1,324,433	Italy	131,658
		Fiscal Years 1964–1973	
Turkey	1,674,853	West Germany	3,382,743
Greece	720,491	United Kingdom	1,665,475
Spain	196,727	Italy	488,197
Norway	123,006	Canada	438,651
		Fiscal Years 1974–1982	
Portugal	347,137	United Kingdom	5,251,219
Turkey	211,832	Netherlands	3,266,439
Greece	147,621	West Germany	3,094,318
Spain	112,052	Belgium	1,948,830

Source: Department of Defense.

[a]Rankings are based on sum of current dollars per program per period.

[b]MAP Program includes: MAP Program, MAP Excess, IMET.

policy emphasis in the region during this period. FMS sales were only $240 million regionally. Australia and Japan were the major FMS program purchasers.

These Asian and Pacific nations were key partners in the U.S. security network for their region. All were parties to major security treaties with the United States and were considered vital to providing a barrier to Communist expansion in this area. A high level of aid was provided to North Asian countries after the outbreak of the Korean War, which accounts for the high level of MAP funding in the region in this period. As the industrialized nations among this group regained their economic strength in the latter part of the period, a greater degree of security assistance came from the FMS sales program. Most of the nations provided very important military bases, or access rights, which facilitated U.S. power projection into their region and increased U.S. deterrent capability accordingly.

Ranking third in distribution of MAP program resources was the Near East and South Asia at more than $1.5 billion. This region received substantially fewer funds than did the previous two regions, reflecting the relative lack of U.S. policy emphasis in this region. The primary recipients of MAP funding were Iran and Pakistan. Saudi

Table 1–2
Leading Program Participants by Region: East Asia and Pacific[a]
(thousands of current U.S. dollars)

MAP Program[b]		*MAP Program[c]*		*FMS (sales) Program Agreements*	
		Fiscal years 1950–1963			
Taiwan	2,537,225			Australia	144,228
South Korea	2,130,030			Japan	73,732
South Vietnam	1,061,105				
Japan	1,001,933				
		Fiscal Years 1964–1973			
		South Vietnam	10,458,182	Australia	922,650
		South Korea	3,209,731	Taiwan	476,088
		Laos	1,039,813	Japan	283,143
		Taiwan	920,048	New Zealand	105,602
		Fiscal Years 1974–1982			
		South Vietnam	4,657,167	Australia	5,093,758
		South Korea	957,065	South Korea	3,862,011
		Cambodia	780,305	Taiwan	2,914,124
		Laos	367,772	Japan	2,476,777

Source: Department of Defense.

[a]Rankings are based on sum of current dollars per program per period.

[b]MAP Program includes: MAP Program, MAP Excess, IMET.

[c]MAP Program includes: MAP Program, MAP Excess, MASF Program, MAP Excess, IMET.

Arabia was the leader in FMS program purchases, which for the region were about $184 million. In all of these cases the MAP funding or FMS purchasing levels were relatively low.

The leading recipients of security assistance, Iran and Pakistan, were seen as especially important to the containment of Soviet expansion into the Persian Gulf and Indian Ocean region. The strategic oil resources of the Gulf states were of particular importance to the Western industrial states. Consequently, Iran was among the states provided with military aid at the beginning of the MAP program in 1949. U.S. interest in maintaining stability in Iran was reflected by continuous support for the Shah of Iran from the early 1950s onward.

Pakistan received most of its security assistance from 1954 on, as the United States became increasingly concerned with Soviet activities in Southwest Asia. Further, after 1954 Pakistan associated itself with SEATO and with the Baghdad Pact. As a result, increased U.S. military assistance to Pakistan was provided as a tangible ele-

Table 1–3
Leading Program Participants by Region: Near East and South Asia[a]
(thousands of current U.S. dollars)

MAP Program[b]		*MAP Program[c]*		*FMS (sales) Program Agreements*	
		Fiscal Years 1950–1963			
Iran	673,208			Saudi Arabia	86,179
Pakistan	650,004			India	52,266
India	66,116			Pakistan	32,557
		Fiscal Years 1964–1973			
Iran	222,597			Iran	3,642,634
Jordan	162,527			Israel	1,525,235
India	50,925			Saudi Arabia	627,812
Pakistan	49,436			Jordan	188,363
		Fiscal Years 1974–1982			
		Israel	5,500,000	Saudi Arabia	22,583,182
		Jordan	354,301	Iran	8,913,001
		Egypt	204,540	Israel	8,240,243
		Tunisia	9,611	Egypt	5,369,169

Source: Department of Defense
[a]Rankings are based on sum of current dollars per program per period.
[b]MAP Program includes: MAP Program, MAP Excess, IMET.
[c]MAP Program includes: MAP Program, MAP Excess, IMET, FMS financing waived (FY 1974–FY 1982).

ment of U.S. support for Pakistan's willingness to align itself directly with the Western collective security network.

Although Saudi Arabia, India, and Pakistan made most of the FMS cash purchases in this period, the amounts involved were modest and were basically aimed at providing a minimum of military capability for local defense forces. The Saudi sales program, while minimal, was considered important to U.S. policymakers as a means of supporting a nation that had vast oil resources and had maintained its distance from the Pan-Arab nationalism stimulated by Egyptian President Nasser.

Ranking fourth and fifth in MAP program and grant training funding were Latin America and Africa at $600 million and $93.5 million respectively. These totals reflect the clear lack of policy emphasis in these regions during this period. The leading MAP program recipients in Latin America were Brazil, Chile, and Peru. FMS sales were about $198 million, and in this region Venezuela and Argentina were the leading FMS program purchasers.

Table 1–4
Leading Program Participants by Region: American Republics[a]
(thousands of current U.S. dollars)

MAP Program[b]		*FMS (sales) Program Agreements*	
	Fiscal Years 1950–1963		
Brazil	237,582	Venezuela	61,181
Chile	84,056	Argentina	47,525
Peru	72,859	Peru	20,777
Colombia	56,085	Brazil	19,217
	Fiscal Years 1964–1973		
Brazil	66,777	Brazil	131,353
Colombia	55,723	Venezuela	114,136
Argentina	45,571	Argentina	84,822
Peru	36,845	Chile	45,186
	Fiscal Years 1974–1982		
El Salvador	95,653	Venezuela	760,399
Honduras	17,835	Brazil	153,142
Bolivia	16,005	Chile	126,314
Paraguay	7,330	Peru	125,742

Source: Department of Defense

[a]Rankings are based on sum of current dollars per program per period.

[b]MAP Program includes: MAP Program, MAP Excess, IMET.

In Latin America the U.S. security assistance program was minimal because most nations were not perceived to be seriously threatened, by either external aggression or internal subversion. This changed after Castro seized power in Cuba. Most Latin American states had governments that were either politically conservative, dominated by an anti-Communist military, or both. As a consequence, most security assistance was used as symbolic support or to meet defense requirements at a level that the U.S. believed was necessary for the security needs of this region. Only the more financially well-off nations, such as Venezuela, could afford to make modest FMS purchases. The leading MAP recipients were those nations in the region that had the more advanced military forces by regional standards. By most standards, however, the level of security assistance provided was minimal, consistent with the U.S. view of the low level of threat to the security of the region.

In Africa the leading MAP program recipient was Ethiopia, followed by Liberia. Had Ethiopia not been a recipient of MAP monies, there would have been only a relatively negligible African program.

Table 1–5
Leading Program Participants by Region: Africa[a]
(thousands of current U.S. dollars)

MAP Program[b]		*FMS (sales) Program Agreements*	
	Fiscal Years 1950–1963		
Ethiopia	84,122	Liberia	1,146
Liberia	2,648	South Africa	925
Zaire	2,420	Ethiopia	663
Senegal	2,167		
	Fiscal Years 1964–1973		
Ethiopia	126,525	Zaire	18,889
Zaire	29,209	Nigeria	3,332
Liberia	6,076	South Africa	2,223
Mali	1,556	Liberia	1,357
	Fiscal Years 1974–1982		
Sudan	54,473	Sudan	230,520
Ethiopia	25,669	Kenya	148,695
Somalia	15,830	Ethiopia	99,171
Kenya	14,247	Zaire	75,503

Source: Department of Defense

[a]Rankings are based on sum of current dollars per program per period.

[b]MAP Program includes: MAP Program, MAP Excess, IMET.

FMS program purchases were also minimal, with Liberia the principal buyer. The entire region's FMS purchases barely exceeded $2.7 million.

U.S. security assistance program levels were consistently low for Africa in this period, as for nearly all of the subsequent periods, because the United States did not perceive a serious threat to its vital interests in this region. Africa was notably underdeveloped, although possessing valuable mineral resources in some cases, but was not seen as at the center of the East–West conflict during these years. Ethiopia, however, was strategically located in northeast Africa, was pro-Western, and provided important military facilities for use by U.S. military forces. Consequently, until 1977, when Ethiopia's government became a Soviet client state, it was by far the leading recipient of American security assistance in Africa.

It should be noted that during this period (FY 1950–FY 1963) most of the relatively advanced equipment provided through the security assistance program went to highly industrialized European nations with the most advanced military forces. This equipment was

Table 1–6
Regional Rankings
(millions of current U.S. dollars)

Grants (MAP/IMET/EXCESS MAP)		FMS (sales) Agreements	
Fiscal Years 1950–1963			
Europe/Canada	18,400	Europe/Canada	2,900
East Asia/Pacific	8,970	East Asia/Pacific	239.6
Near East/South Asia	1,570	American Republics	198
American Republics	600.3	Near East/South Asia	184.1
Africa	93.5	Africa	2.7
Fiscal Years 1964–1973			
East Asia/Pacific[a]	19,170[b]	Europe/Canada	7,700
Europe/Canada	2,770	Near East/South Asia	6,170
Near East/South Asia	582.8	East Asia/Pacific	1,930
American Republics	426.9	American Republics	466
Africa	167.6	Africa	25.1
Fiscal Years 1974–1982			
Near East/South Asia	6,100[c]	Near East/South Asia	51,400
East Asia/Pacific	3,020[d]	Europe/Canada	24,100
Europe/Canada	819.5	East Asia/Pacific	16,800
American Republics	193.8	American Republics	1,610
Africa	134.59	Africa	725.1

Source: Defense Security Assistance Agency.
[a]MASF included in this region.
[b]Excluding $2.25 billion MAP/MASF Excess.
[c]Includes FMS financing: MAP total was $391.5 million.
[d]Excluding $153.007 million MASF/MAP Excess.

provided both from new procurement and from stocks "excess" to U.S. requirements, including aircraft, armor, heavy artillery, and some naval craft, spare parts, and support equipment.

Developing nations received less sophisticated equipment during these years, appropriate with the lower absorption capability of their military forces. While it is true that important allies received weapons and ammunition that were excess to U.S. military requirements, the primary determinants of which countries received what kinds of equipment were the recipient's level of military sophistication and absorption capacity and its immediate defense requirements. Thus, outside of Europe, most recipients of military security assistance received equipment that dated from World War II and was generally less capable. Furthermore, spare parts, support equipment, and training services comprised the largest percentage of the value of military items transferred by the U.S. government to all regions during the period, including Europe.

The Vietnam War and the Security Assistance Program, 1963–1973

It is an understatement to say that the Vietnam conflict had a profound effect on domestic support for the U.S. security assistance program. The Vietnam conflict dominated U.S. foreign and defense policy considerations from 1963 to 1973, and had a profound effect on domestic support for the U.S. security assistance program. The Vietnam conflict was seen by the Kennedy, Johnson, and, ultimately, Nixon administration, as a model case of Soviet or Communist-inspired "wars of national liberation." It was seen by many in Washington as an opportunity to demonstrate that the United States could meet such a challenge through an aggressive program of military and economic assistance, buttressed by the power of U.S. armed forces themselves, if necessary.

After the successful rehabilitation of Europe and the containment of communism in South Korea, U.S. policymakers were able to devote more attention to the emerging Third World, its problems, and the consequences of those problems. The dissolution of old colonial relationships created new political instability in various regions outside Europe and new opportunities for the Soviets to exploit the ensuing turmoil to their advantage. The Cuban missile crisis of 1962 was a frightening and sobering experience for both the Soviet Union and the United States. After its resolution, an international political atmosphere was created that suggested that in the future East–West conflict would be confined to a lower level, and greater emphasis was therefore placed on competition in the Third World through such instruments as military and economic aid.

Although the threat of future confrontation with the Soviets did not vanish after the Cuban missile crisis, the fact that no war had broken out in Europe since 1945 and that peace between East and West had been maintained since the Korean War led to a greater sense of security in the United States in the early 1960s. It also fostered the belief that the security assistance programs, while important, need not be funded at the levels of the height of the Cold War.

Other international events besides the Vietnam conflict troubled U.S. policymakers in the 1960s and early 1970s. Africa was politically unstable, with many new nations emerging from former colonial empires. The efforts of Castro to export his form of communism in Latin America led to various direct U.S. responses in the 1960s. These ranged from stressing economic development through the Alliance for Progress to direct military intervention in the Dominican Republic in 1965 to forestall what President Lyndon Johnson believed was an attempt to impose a Communist-dominated regime.

In the Middle East, war broke out between Israel and key Arab states in 1967, and the enmity between these neighboring countries intensified in the wake of Israel's military victory. Subsequently, the United States began transfers of more sophisticated weaponry to Israel to help it maintain a military balance with the more numerous Arab forces. At the same time the United States became increasingly involved in efforts to achieve a Middle East peace.

Proof that the Cold War was not over came in 1968 when Soviet and Warsaw Pact troops crushed a budding democratic movement in Czechoslovakia. While this Communist military action was condemned in the West, it was clear that the United States and its allies were unprepared to go to war with the Soviets over actions taken in a country that was clearly within the Soviet sphere of influence.

Events such as these, however, did not lead to substantial increases in funding levels for security assistance. In the 1960s most security assistance went to the less developed Third World, whose absorption capacities were limited. Congress increasingly saw the program's military elements as less necessary than economic and developmental assistance and the program's funding continued to decline. Had it not been for the Vietnam conflict, the MAP program levels would likely have fallen even more precipitously than they did during the early years of this period. By 1963 a shift was already in process away from the grant MAP program to the cash and credit Foreign Military Sales (FMS) program. With the help of the Marshall Plan the economies of most industrialized nations in Western Europe had recovered. Their governments were now better able to pay for needed military items without grants from the United States. U.S. policymakers, particularly in Congress, made clear that they expected major allies to do just that. In Asia, Japan and Taiwan advanced economically and increased their purchases of U.S. weaponry, as did other allies such as Australia.

These trends away from MAP and toward FMS accelerated into the early 1970s. In 1969 President Nixon announced the "Nixon Doctrine," setting forth the concept of having Third World powers assume greater responsibility for maintaining regional stability. The doctrine had its genesis in the Vietnam experience, where the United States had attempted to carry the burden of a regional war almost singlehandedly. Under the Nixon Doctrine the United States would use its security assistance resources to bolster the military power of key regional states to the extent that those states were willing and able to preserve regional peace without direct U.S. military involvement. A large military sales program to Iran, for example, was justified on the grounds that it would enable the Shah of Iran to provide protection for Persian Gulf oil—enhancing Western security and reducing the degree of direct American military involvement necessary to achieve the same end.

Before such a program shift could be fully implemented, the United States experienced the great disillusionment of Vietnam. Despite the expenditure of tremendous resources in support of a friendly government, a determined foe prevailed, and regional peace is still not restored. The Vietnam conflict, more than any other event during this period, drove the allocation of security assistance program outlays, and reshaped attitudes toward security assistance in general. The degree to which Vietnam and Vietnam-related expenditures dominated the security assistance programs in this period (1963–1973) is evident in the regional distribution of program assets.

From 1963 through 1973 the East Asia and Pacific region ranked first in the regular MAP program account at over $3.8 billion (not including "excess" program items). But this dominance in the basic MAP account was overshadowed by the more than $15 billion provided to Vietnam, Laos, South Korea, and Thailand during this time through a special military assistance service fund (MASF) established outside of the regular MAP program. The MASF grant program of military aid and training far outstripped MAP accounts collectively from FY 1966 when it was established through its peak year of FY 1973. The MASF program was authorized and appropriated through Department of Defense authorization and appropriation bills (FY 1966–FY 1975), while the regular security assistance program were authorized and appropriated through the annual foreign assistance acts. Beginning in 1968 the FMS program was authorized through the Foreign Military Sales Act of 1968 and subsequent amendments.

The MASF program to aid in the Vietnam effort was clearly a security assistance program despite its special nature. It provided grant military assistance to Vietnam and other free nations in Asia to help with the war effort. Because of its size, it probably played an important role in the reaction against military aid programs in the United States because the Vietnam conflict was resolved in a fashion that left considerable bitterness in the United States over the resources expended in that conflict and the apparent futility of the effort made (see table 1–7).

The sizes of the MAP program elements in other regions show its decline in comparison to the high levels of the early 1950s (see tables 1–1 through 1–5 and table 1–6). In Europe and Canada—which ranked second during this period—over $2.7 billion in grant military aid and training was provided. The principal recipients were Turkey, Greece, and Spain—nations in which the U.S. maintained important military bases. At the same time the FMS purchasers in this region were led by West Germany and the United Kingdom, two major NATO partners. Regionally, FMS purchases exceeded $7.7 billion. FMS program purchases in the East Asia and Pacific region were substantially lower at $1.9 billion. The primary purchasers were Australia and Taiwan, nations with whom the United States had long-standing security agreements.

The Near East and South Asia region ranked third in its share of MAP program funds—FY 1964–FY 1973—at a level in excess of $582 million. Principal recipients were Iran and Jordan, states that had pro-Western governments deemed important to U.S. regional policy interests. FMS purchases by this region, however, increased significantly during these years to a level of about $6.2 billion, a level approaching that of the Europe and Canada region. Principal purchasers were Iran, Saudi Arabia, and Israel. This reflected the policy perspective of President Nixon's doctrine of building up friendly regional states through military aid and the increased American commitment to Israel after the 1967 Arab–Israeli War.

Latin America ranked fourth in MAP program and training during this period at $426.9 million. Principal recipient countries were Brazil, Columbia, and Argentina. In FMS purchases the region also ranked fourth at $466 million, with Brazil, Venezuela, and Argentina the primary buyers. These totals reflect continued U.S. security association with those Latin states that have the larger military establishments as well as continued U.S. restraint in expanding military expenditures in an area where the Cuban threat seemed effectively contained.

Africa ranked last in MAP program accounts at $167.6 million, with Ethiopia, a long-term client of the United States, and Zaire as the principal recipient nations. The leading FMS purchaser was Zaire which received greater U.S. support in the wake of the Congolese conflict of the 1960s. Regional FMS purchases were $25.1 million. The relatively low levels of security assistance program funding for Africa and Latin America reflect the policy priority placed on Viet-

Table 1–7
MAP Funding Compared to MASF Funding for Key Asian Countries, FY 1964–FY 1973
(thousands of current U.S. dollars)

	Vietnam		*South Korea*		*Laos*		*Thailand*		
Fiscal years	*MAP*[a]	*MASF*[b]	*MAP*[a]	*MASF*[b]	*MAP*[a]	*MASF*[b]	*MAP*[a]	*MASF*[b]	*Fiscal years*
1964	184,817		122,493		21,375		32,697		1964
1965	237,862		111,680		39,872		25,651		1965
1966	98,380	551,275	161,758	36,849	51,491	8,740	30,249	16,417	1966
1967		647,440	169,423	99,589	51,820	29,315	21,027	43,221	1967
1968		964,887	253,469	110,346		80,701		84,711	1968
1969		1,250,762	137,960	294,580		88,839		86,314	1969
1970		1,469,019	136,654	181,523		136,503		91,647	1970
1971		1,863,827	291,937	232,424		194,483		77,750	1971
1972		2,292,034	154,505	319,513		279,108		99,139	1972
1973		3,246,675	150,365	149,844		274,485	41,816		1973

Source: Defense Security Assistance Agency.

Note: This table illustrates the high level of MASF funds allocated to Asia during the Vietnam War period—funds that would not have been allocated at such a high level had the war not provided the basis for such a program.

[a]MAP category includes MAP program and training account only and not excess account.

[b]MASF category includes program account and training only, not excess account; MASF began in FY 1966.

nam during these years and the traditional low level of U.S. involvement in African internal affairs.

The Security Assistance Program in the Recent Period, 1973–1982

By 1973 the negative domestic political fallout from the Vietnam war had accelerated the trend away from support for the MAP program and had eroded congressional support for security assistance generally. During the period from 1973 to 1982 the security assistance program underwent a critical reevaluation by the Congress and various legislative changes led to modifications in overall program levels for particular countries and specific accounts.

The 1973 Arab–Israeli War and the Arab oil embargo, and general instability in the Middle East and Horn of Africa set the context for the security assistance program in this period. Also of concern to U.S. policymakers was the increase in the use of Soviet proxies in Africa, including Cuban troops in Angola during the civil war there in the mid-1970s, and Soviet and other Communist advisors in Ethiopia after a pro-Soviet government seized power in that country in 1977.

Two very significant events affecting U.S. interests occurred in the latter part of the period. In 1979 the pro-Western Shah of Iran was overthrown by intensely anti-American and anti-Western forces determined to export Islamic fundamentalist revolution throughout the Middle East. Later that same year the Soviet Union invaded and occupied Afghanistan, the first direct military intervention by the Soviets in a nation outside its traditional sphere of influence in Eastern Europe since the Second World War.

These events caused the United States to place far greater emphasis on strategic planning in the Middle East and the Persian Gulf. U.S. administrations also intensified their involvement in the Middle East peace process. A positive outcome of these efforts was the Egyptian–Israeli peace treaty worked out at Camp David by President Carter. This policy emphasis led to greatly increased security assistance for the region, with more than half of U.S. security assistance program funds and weapons sales directed to this region during these years.

Arms sales increased to Arab states that the United States considered moderate, especially Saudi Arabia. United States interests in bolstering the Saudi defensive capability were tangibly illustrated by FMS cash sales of advanced F-15 fighter aircraft in 1978 and E-3A

Airborne Warning and Control System (AWACS) planes and F-15 enhancements in 1981. Efforts to foster closer Saudi–U.S. defense cooperation increased after the Iranian revolution in 1979, and the outbreak of war between Iran and Iraq in the fall of 1980 threatened both the flow of oil from the Persian Gulf and the political stability and security of friendly Arab states in the area.

Specific legislative enactments in this period made major changes in the traditional security assistance program. In 1976 Congress voted the phaseout of the MAP program. Since September 30, 1977, MAP funds must be specifically authorized by Congress. Most use of MAP funds in subsequent years has been to wind up existing MAP program operations, and grant MAP has been authorized in unique and limited circumstances.

At the same time that Congress called for the phaseout of MAP in the International Assistance and Arms Export Control Act of 1976, it also created the International Military Education and Training (IMET) program to carry on the training functions previously conducted through the MAP program. Military education and training under IMET encompasses formal and informal instruction of foreign military personnel in the United States and overseas by officers or employees of the United States, contract technicians, contractors, or through correspondence courses, technical educational information publications or other media. It also involves orientation, training aids and military advice to foreign military forces. Unless the president justifies such training to Congress, no IMET training may be conducted outside of the United States.

The intent of IMET, as with its MAP predecessor, is to foster effective utilization by recipient countries of U.S.-supplied defense articles and services and to encourage better understanding and cooperation between the United States and foreign country participants. Since the inception of the grant military training program in 1950, over 500,000 foreign personnel from approximately 100 nations have participated.

With the winding down of the MAP program after the Vietnam conflict and the increase in the use of the FMS program to enhance U.S. objectives, the regional totals of MAP and the grant training program for FY 1974 to FY 1982 (whether part of MAP or IMET) show a notable decline from previous periods (see tables 1–5 and 1–6).

East Asia and the Pacific region led in MAP program and training funds at over $3 billion (not including an additional $1.76 billion in MASF program items). Apart from Vietnam, principal recipient nations were South Korea, Cambodia, and Thailand, all longstanding regional allies. In FMS program purchases, the region ranked third, with sales of $16.8 billion. Principal purchasers were Australia, South Korea, and Taiwan, reflecting their enhanced ability to pay for modern military equipment.

Europe and Canada ranked third in MAP program and training funding during this period at a level in excess of $819.5 million. Principal country recipients were Portugal and Turkey who provided important U.S. military bases. In FMS purchases this region ranked second, at a level of over $24.1 billion. The United Kingdom and West Germany were the clear leaders in purchases.

In the Near East and South Asia region MAP program and training funds were nearly $393 million. The primary MAP recipient was Jordan, reflecting the continuing U.S. support for that moderate Arab state. Israel received $5.5 billion in de facto grants through waiver of repayment of loans covering this amount of its FMS purchases. This region was the clear leader in FMS program purchases, at a level of $51.4 billion. Saudi Arabia, Iran, and Israel were the leading FMS program purchasers. Saudi Arabia's position as the leading purchaser reflects U.S. efforts to bring that nation into closer association with U.S. collective security efforts in the region and assure continued Western access to its major oil reserves.

Latin America and Africa ranked fourth and fifth in MAP program and training funding respectively during this period, with Latin America receiving $193.8 million and Africa $134.6 million. The principal Latin American recipient of MAP program funds in this period has been El Salvador, because of the Reagan administration response to insurgent threats to that country. FMS sales for Latin America amounted to about $1.6 billion for this period. Primary purchasers were Venezuela, Brazil, and Chile—traditionally leading buyers in this region.

In Africa the MAP program and training level was over $134.5 million. Principal recipient nations were Sudan and Ethiopia. The FMS program for Africa exceeded $725 million, with Sudan and Kenya the principal purchasers, reflecting increased U.S. concern with threats to Sudan by Soviet proxies and efforts to maintain close political ties with pro-Western Kenya.

As the FMS cash and credit program grew rapidly during the mid-1970s to 1980s, Congress placed a number of restriction on sales to specific countries because of its concern with human rights or disagreement with the policies of particular governments. In this period Congress became particularly assertive in expressing its policy views on security assistance to certain countries. Many members felt that the Vietnam experience had shown that greater selectivity should be displayed in providing such support to foreign governments. There were clear institutional and philosophical differences on this point between the executive and legislative branches. But in the wake of the Watergate scandal and the ascendent belief that presidential authority had to be effectively balanced by Congress, the legislative branch began to make policy determinations in legislation regarding security assistance that heretofore had often been left to the president's discretion.

As it became clear that the FMS program was becoming the predominant element in the security assistance program, Congress passed a number of legislative oversight measures to give it a more direct role in the arms sales process. Among these measures were the authority after 1974 for Congress to veto a major arms sale by passage of a concurrent resolution, various detailed reporting requirements on prospective arms transfers, and funding restrictions on transfers to specific countries. Statutory limitations on transfers between program accounts were also tightened.

The Near East and South Asia region became the center of focus for U.S. programs during this period. The Arab–Israeli war of 1973 and the related oil embargo against the United States raised new policy concerns about maintaining access to the oil resources of this strategic region while achieving a lasting peace between Israel and its Arab neighbors.

To foster the end of bolstering the position of the United States in the Near East and South Asia, a massive arms sales program was undertaken through the FMS program. Israel was rearmed and special funding arrangements were established to enable it to bear the cost of increased military purchases. Starting with the FY 1974 aid bill a substantial amount of Israel's FMS credit purchases were waived. Since then $5.5 billion in such waivers have been made. Recently (FY 1982), Egypt was provided with $200 million and the Sudan $50 million in such FMS waivers.

Israel was also given the opportunity, beginning in 1976, to service its FMS debts through "concessional" financing whereby the total loan period was extended to thirty years with repayment of principal on new FMS loans deferred for the first ten years. Subsequently, this concessional formula was extended to other friendly nations, specifically Turkey, Greece, the Sudan, and Egypt. These measures were undertaken to support nations considered important to U.S. national security interests because of important military bases they provided or their support for a Mid-East peace process but who were having problems in purchasing necessary military equipment.

A more recent Reagan administration initiative in this area was a proposal to offer "direct" FMS credits at interest rates as low as 3 to 5 percent to countries that would have serious difficulty in paying market interest rates on their FMS loans. Congress continues to review this proposal. In the interim it has attempted to ease the financial burden on needy recipients with a combination of grants and guaranteed loans at market interest rates.

An examination of the security assistance program for the period (FY 1974–FY 1982) demonstrates the degree to which the FMS program has come to dominate the entire program. As a result of the large increase in the price of the oil, many friendly states in the Near East and South Asia region are able to pay cash for FMS purchases. Thus, countries like Iran and Saudi Arabia have made large purchases of major U.S. weapon systems (although the Iranian program ended in 1979 after the Shah's overthrow). The stated U.S. objective in selling this equipment has been not only to increase the defensive capability of the recipient state, but to foster sufficient regional stability that the prospects for a comprehensive Middle East peace might be advanced.

Iran, Afghanistan, the Carter Doctrine, and the Rapid Deployment Force

Large FMS cash sales to Iran and Afghanistan have not always led to the outcomes sought by U.S. policymakers. In 1979 the Shah of Iran was overthrown and replced by a government very hostile to the United States and to its friends in the region. This led to increased skepticism about the long-range efficacy of the FMS program for advancing U.S. interests. Yet policymakers have countered by citing the experience of Western Europe after World War II, when the massive military aid program contributed to stabilizing a critical region. In addition, it has been argued that by supporting a major military buildup of Egypt after it signed a peace treaty with Israel the United States has laid the foundation of a security structure in the Middle East that, over time, may help lead to long-sought peace and stability within the area.

Regional instability, exacerbated by the Iranian revolution, however, has led the United States to become more directly involved in this area. When the Soviet Union invaded Afghanistan in 1979, apparently attempting to strengthen its ability to influence events in the vital Persian Gulf oil region, President Carter announced what has come to be called the Carter Doctrine. Simply stated, the Carter

Doctrine enunciates a U.S. commitment to oppose subversion and aggression in the Persian Gulf and Middle East directly.

To give strength to this declaration, the Carter administration established a Rapid Deployment Force (RDF) to enable U.S. forces to be sent into the Persian Gulf region quickly should circumstances warrant it. To make this military commitment more credible, the United States obtained base access agreements with Kenya, Somalia, and Oman for the use of U.S. military forces. Other informal arrangements were undertaken in conjunction with Egypt to obtain permission to use local military facilities in specific contingencies.

The provision of various combinations of security assistance has played an important role in obtaining or maintaining access to important overseas military facilities. This has been true in NATO's southern region—in Greece, Turkey, Portugal, and Spain—and also in Asia, particularly in Japan and the Philippines. As the United States seeks to maintain the flexibility to project military power into key regions, the use of security assistance to help retain access to bases in strategically located nations is likely to continue to a significant degree, although most nations are more reluctant today to provide access to and use of military facilities in an unrestricted manner regardless of the levels of U.S. security assistance. (For major international events that have affected the evolution of the program, see appendix B.)

To increase program flexibility, the Carter administration sought and the Reagan administration obtained the creation of a Special Defense Acquisition Fund (SDAF) in 1981. The SDAF is a revolving fund separate from other accounts under the control of the Department of Defense. The purpose of the SDAF is to finance the acquisition of defense articles and services in anticipation of their transfer under authority of the Arms Export Control Act, the Foreign Assistance Act of 1961 (as amended), or as otherwise authorized by law, to eligible countries or international organizations. The SDAF's objectives are to permit rapid supply of high-demand defense articles without adverse impact on the combat readiness of U.S. forces and to promote even rates of production and reduce procurement costs for both the U.S. and foreign governments.

A security assistance program that has existed under various names for years (including "defense support," "supporting assistance," and "security supporting assistance") that is an adjunct to the military assistance and sales programs previously discussed is the Economic Support Fund (ESF)—so named since 1978. The ESF is a flexible instrument that provides funds, on either a loan or grant basis, to be used for various economic purposes, including balance of payments support, financing of infrastructure and other capital projects, and support for development projects which directly benefit the poor. Recently the bulk of ESF funds have gone to the Middle East to deal with Israel's serious balance of payments problems and to aid development projects in Egypt. Because ESF funds help to free up matching amounts of local funds within a recipient country, they make expenditures of local funds by that nation for other military or economic purposes more cost-effective.

Historic Relationship of Security Assistance Program to Other Elements of the U.S. Budget

There appears to be no direct relationship between the gross national product growth per capita and that of the security assistance program (see figure 1–1). This is true for both foreign military assistance and foreign economic assistance. Neither the amounts of military assistance nor of economic assistance programs per capita have paralleled the growth in the GNP per capita. The growth in federal government transfer payments[1] per capita, however, has tended to parallel the growth in GNP per capita. And, except for a part of the Korean War, the amounts of federal government transfer payments per capita have always exceeded those per capita amounts for foreign military assistance and foreign economic assistance.

The data in figure 1–1 also suggest that there has been no direct relationship between the growth and cyclic variations in the U.S. economy and the amounts made available for security assistance programs. Rather, as the previous discussion of funding levels (FY 1950–FY 1982) and regional allocations of security assistance resources indicates, international developments have driven the provision of specific assistance to various nations to support U.S. foreign and defense policy objectives.

When one considers further that Department of Defense budget authority has always greatly exceeded security assistance program appropriations, it is evident that security assistance has not constituted a significant portion of the total federal budget. For example, the FY 1950 MAP component was $1.3 billion compared to $14.1 billion in budget authority for the Department of Defense (see table 1–8). With the onset of the Korean War these numbers radically changed: the FY 1951 MAP component was $5.2 billion while $47.5 billion in budget authority was given to DOD, and the MAP program peaked in the FY 1952 budget at $5.7 billion, while DOD budget authority rose to $60.2 billion.

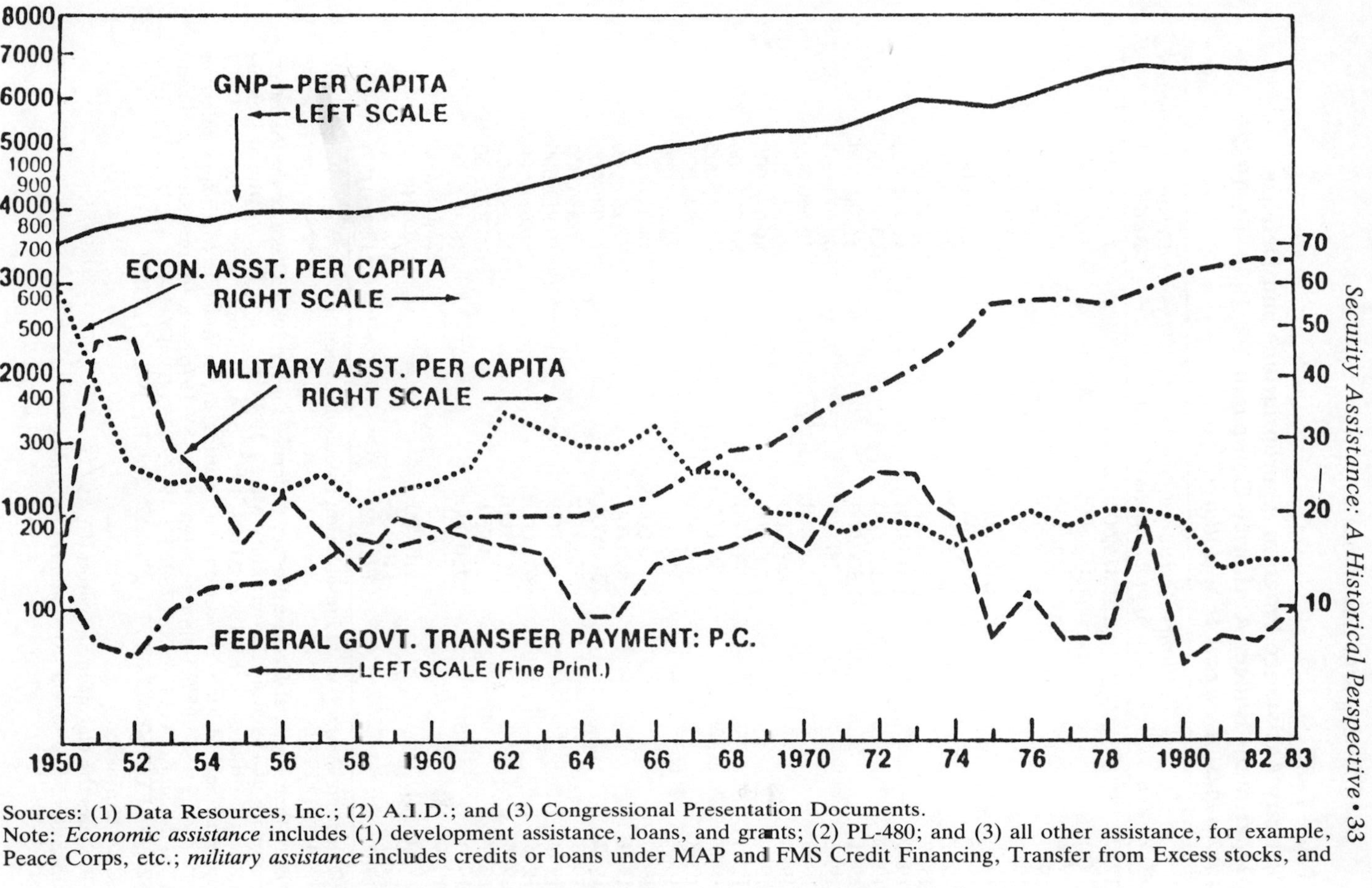

Sources: (1) Data Resources, Inc.; (2) A.I.D.; and (3) Congressional Presentation Documents.
Note: *Economic assistance* includes (1) development assistance, loans, and grants; (2) PL-480; and (3) all other assistance, for example, Peace Corps, etc.; *military assistance* includes credits or loans under MAP and FMS Credit Financing, Transfer from Excess stocks, and

Figure 1–1. U.S. Economic Indicators *(1972 constant dollars)*

Table 1–8
Military Assistance Program Appropriations and Defense Department Budget Authority Compared, FY 1950–FY 1982
(thousands of current U.S. dollars)

Fiscal Year	*Military Assistance Program Appropriations*[a]	*Defense Department Budget Authority*[b]
1950	1,314,000	14,086,000
1951	5,222,500	47,534,000
1952	5,744,000	60,196,000
1953	4,219,800	48,603,000
1954	3,230,000	34,319,000
1955	1,192,700	30,425,000
1956	1,022,200	32,791,000
1957	2,017,000	35,916,000
1958	1,340,000	36,971,000
1959	1,515,000	41,402,000
1960	1,300,000	40,907,000
1961	1,800,000	41,386,000
1962	1,600,000	48,014,000
1963	1,325,000	49,560,000
1964	1,000,000	49,627,000
1965	1,130,000	49,058,000
1966	1,470,000	63,555,000
1967	792,000	72,177,000
1968	500,000	76,342,000
1969	375,000	76,905,000
1970	350,000	74,083,000
1971	690,000	71,159,000
1972	500,000	75,006,000
1973	553,100[c]	77,555,000
1974	450,000	80,991,000
1975	475,000	85,661,000
1976[d]	252,200	111,736,000
1977	264,550	108,338,000
1978	220,000[e]	115,322,000
1979	83,275	125,004,000
1980	110,000[c]	142,621,000
1981	110,200[c]	178,400,000
1982	171,412	214,100,000

[a]Data from Congressional Presentation Document. Security Assistance Programs FY 1984, pp. 11–12.

[b]Data from National Defense Budget Estimates for FY 1982, Office of the Assistant Secretary of Defense (Comptroller), March 1981, p. 5 and Ibid. Nàtional Defense Budget Estimates for FY 1983, March 1982, p. 4. Amounts appropriated for IMET (International Military Education and Training) are *included* in MAP appropriations *prior* to FY 1976. IMET appropriations from FY 1976 were (in thousands of current U.S. dollars): FY 1976: $28,750; FY 1977: $25,000; FY 1978: $30,000; FY 1979: $27,900; FY 1980: $25,000; FY 1981: $28,300; FY 1982: $42,000.

[c]CRA Limitation.

[d]Includes the transitional quarter (FY 197T).

[e]Includes $40,200,000 subsequently rescinded.

After the Korean War ended, the MAP program appropriation stabilized in excess of $1 billion per year through 1965. DOD budget authority dropped no lower than $30.4 billion (FY 1955) and generally increased in the following years—thereby increasing the relative gap in funds available for the DOD programs compared to that for MAP and the security assistance program.

The MAP appropriation reached its post-Korean war high in FY 1957 at $2 billion. After that year it continued a general decline for most of the following fiscal years, never rising above the $792 million level after FY 1967. Even if the FMS credit program appropriations (see table 1–9) are added to those of MAP after FY 1968, along with

Table 1–9
Foreign Military Sales (FMS) Credit Program Appropriations and Defense Department Budget Authority Compared, FY 1969–FY 1982
(thousands of current U.S. dollars)

Fiscal Year	*FMS Credit Program Appropriations*[a]	*Defense Department Budget Authority*[b]
1969	296,000	76,905,000
1970	70,000	74,083,000
1971	700,000[c]	71,159,000
1972	400,000	75,006,000
1973	400,000[d]	77,555,000
1974	2,525,000[e]	80,991,000
1975	300,000	85,661,000
1976[f]	1,205,000	111,376,000
1977	740,000	108,338,000
1978	675,850	115,322,000
1979[g]	1,024,500	125,004,000
1980	645,000[d]	142,621,000
1981	500,000[d]	178,400,000
1982	750,000	214,100,000

Note: Prior to FY 1969 Military Assistance Program (MAP) included FMS Credit Program totals.

[a]Data from Congressional Presentation Document Security Assistance Programs FY 1984, p. 10.

[b]Data from National Defense Budget Estimates for FY 1982, Office of the Assistant Secretary of Defense (Comptroller), March 1981, p. 5 and Ibid. National Defense Budget Estimates for FY 1983, March 1982, p. 4.

[c]Includes $500,000 for Israel authorized by P.L. 91–441 and appropriated by P.L. 91–665.

[d]CRA Limitation.

[e]Includes $2,200,000 for Emergency Security Assistance requested, authorized and appropriated for Israel.

[f]Includes transitional quarter (FY 197T).

[g]Includes supplemental for Israel and Egypt.

Table 1–10
Economic Support Fund (ESF) Appropriations and Defense Department Budget Authority Compared, FY 1964–FY 1982
(thousands of current U.S. dollars)

Fiscal Year	*Economic Support Fund Appropriations*[a]	*Defense Department Budget Authority*[b]
1964	330,000	49,627,000
1965	401,000	49,058,000
1966	684,000	63,555,000
1967	690,000	72,177,000
1968	600,000	76,342,000
1969	365,000	76,905,000
1970	395,000	74,083,000
1971	414,000	71,159,000
1972	550,000	75,006,000
1973	600,000	77,555,000
1974	611,500	80,991,000
1975	1,200,000	85,661,000
1976	1,739,900	95,508,000
197T	279,700	23,022,000
1977	1,757,700[c]	108,338,000
1978	2,219,300	115,322,000
1979	2,282,000	125,004,000
1980	1,942,100[d]	142,621,000
1981	2,104,500[d]	178,400,000
1982	2,576,000	214,100,000

[a]Data from Congressional Presentation Document, Security Assistance Programs FY 1984, p. 10.

[b]Data from National Budget Estimates for FY 1982, Office of the Assistant Secretary of Defense (Comptroller), March 1981, p. 5, and Ibid., National Defense Budget Estimate for FY 1983, March 1982, p. 4.

[c]Includes $300,000 for Portugal; also $20,000 for Lebanon, authorized as Disaster Assistance, but appropriated in the SSA account.

[d]CRA Limitation.

the Economic Support Fund (ESF) appropriations (see table 1–10) from the FY 1964 budget forward, it is still clear that Defense Department budget authority far surpasses these aggregate appropriations in any given fiscal year.

Indeed, adding the appropriations figures for MAP, IMET, FMS credits, and the Economic Support Fund results in a total for FY 1982 of $3.5 billion. That figure represents a historic low for the security assistance program in comparison to the budget authority of the Defense Department, which for FY 1982 was $214 billion. Even adjusting the earlier figures for inflation would not alter the basic point that historically security assistance programs have not constituted a significant proportion of either the DOD budget or of the overall Federal budget.[2]

Data on the grant program element, presented in figure 1–2 demonstrate that the funding levels for this portion of the security assistance program have tended to track major international policy actions by the United States. The grant program was at its height during the early 1950s when NATO and Europe were being rearmed and the Korean War was being fought. After this period it came down in phases until 1963 when the massive effort for Vietnam (later including MASF) led to a sharp increase in levels once again. After FY 1974 levels and the end of the Vietnam war, the grant program dropped dramatically, with an increase occurring in the early 1980s. Thus, today, the grant program bears little relationship in size to the program of the early 1950s. It is substantially smaller, especially when adjusted for inflation.

Data on the FMS credit program shows that this program has also followed the course of U.S. policy emphasis overseas. As figure 1–3 makes evident, the program was small until the period after the

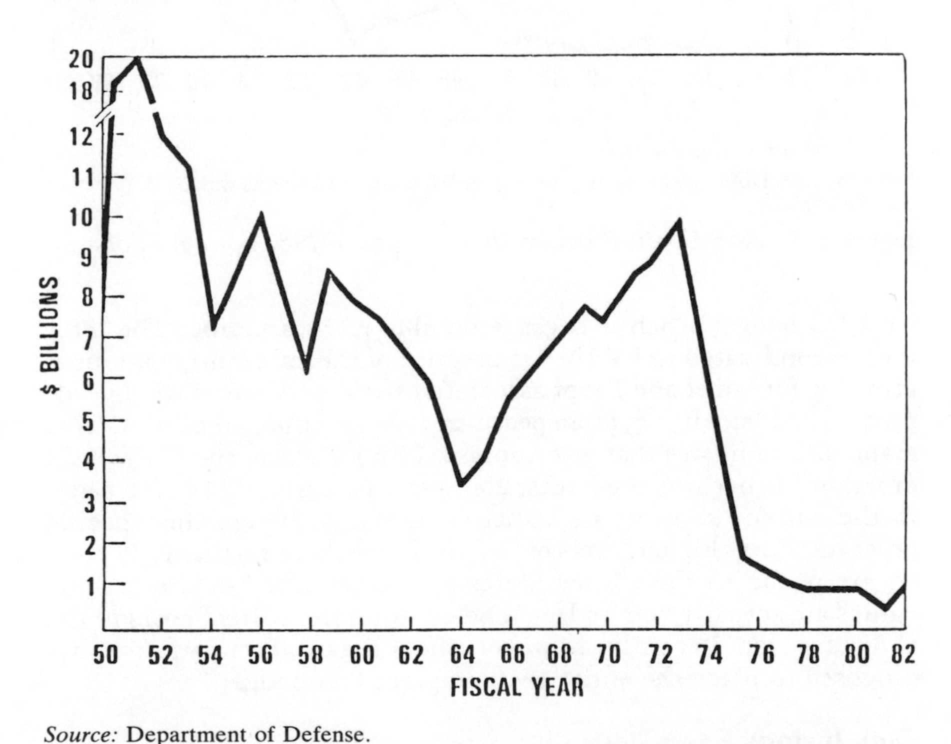

Source: Department of Defense.

Note: Includes MAP, MAP Excess Program, MASF, MASF Excess Program, IMET, MASF Training, and FMS credits waived (FY 1974–FY 1982 only).

Figure 1–2. Grant Program *(billions of FY 1982 constant dollars)*

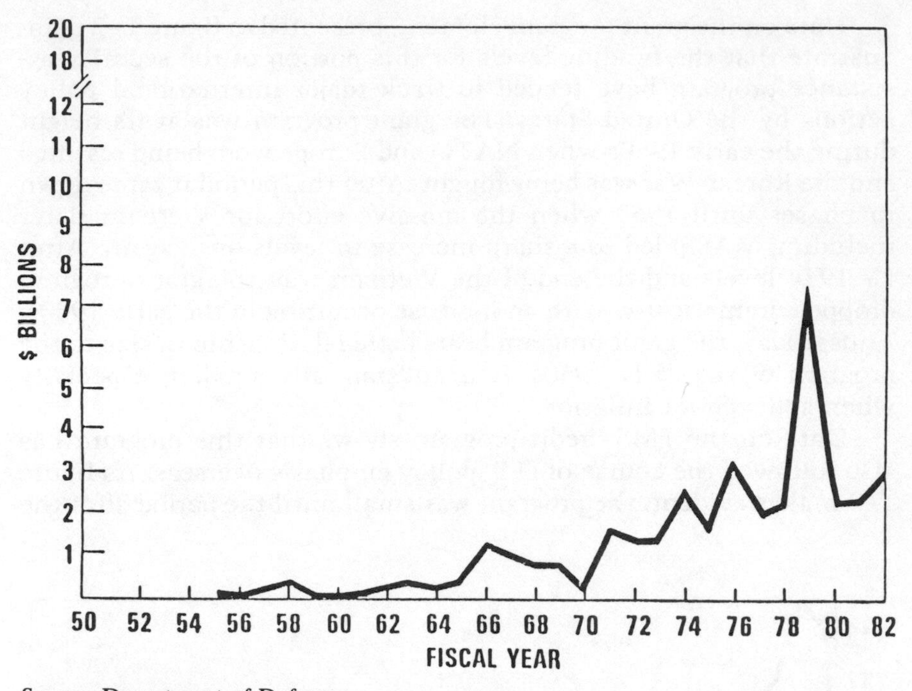

Source: Department of Defense.

Note: Includes Direct and Guaranty financing. Excludes FMS credits waived (FY 1974–FY 1982 only).

Figure 1–3. FMS Credit Program *(billions of FY 1982 constant dollars)*

FY 1970 budget when it began a notable growth period. The large increase indicated in FY 1979 is because of the substantial amounts provided for Israel and Egypt associated with the Camp David peace process and Israeli–Egyptian peace treaty that emerged from it. This graph also indicates that, even adjusted for inflation, the FMS credit program has become the largest element (apart from FMS cash sales) in the current security assistance program. Although this specific program shows higher levels of "funding" (because regular FMS credits are repaid to the United States at market interest rates), these values are actually "off budget" and do not reflect direct costs to the U.S. taxpayer. Recently, however, the Reagan administration has proposed to place the entire FMS program "on budget."

Conclusions

This historical review of the security assistance program indicates that the levels of the program have risen and fallen in relation to major international crises perceived by U.S. policymakers to require use of the program to serve important national security interests. From the formation of NATO and the establishment of the Military Assistance Program in 1949 through the waging of the Korean War and U.S. association with various nations through mutual security pacts in the 1950s, the security assistance program was seen by policymakers as a valuable instrument in the promotion of collective security throughout the globe. It was viewed as a viable means to help others help the United States to support the ultimate objective of preserving world peace, as well as a less costly alternative to direct military involvement, both financially and politically.

As the threat of crisis in Europe passed and that region regained its economic viability and became politically stable once again, U.S. concerns focused on Asia. In the wake of the fall of China to the Communists and the Korean War, U.S. policymakers addressed the new threat of wars of national liberation. Security assistance was seen by U.S. policymakers as a potentially valuable tool to support nation-building in developing regions. Vietnam became, in the U.S. public's mind, the test of that thesis.

Because of the amount of security assistance resources, not to mention U.S. military personnel and power, that was used to wage the Vietnam conflict, the outcome of that effort was bound to shape attitudes toward the viability of the security assistance program in supporting U.S. national objectives. As a consequence of the profound disillusionment that set in after the Vietnam conflict concluded without securing the U.S. objective of preserving the government it had supported, the security assistance program underwent close congressional review and a number of changes in it resulted.

In the 1970s, as the MAP program was phased down and the FMS cash and credit program replaced it as the principal element of security assistance, Congress placed increasing restrictions on program authority and enacted a legislative veto over major arms sales.

An increasing number of the weapons transferred to Third World states since the early 1970s through the FMS program are newer and more advanced versions—in relative terms—than the vintage World War II and Korean War era equipment provided to such nations in the earlier years of the security assistance program. Such transactions stimulated a good deal of the controversy between the executive and legislative branches. This was especially the case when the United States seemed to be fostering regional conflicts by supplying arms to countries friendly to the United States but hostile to non-Communist neighbors in their region, or when the arms sales appeared to undermine a Third World nation's prospects for economic development. Others saw arms sales through the FMS program as an effective way to buildup regional clients to help share the burden of keeping regional peace. This was true of the Nixon and Ford administrations, and, to a lesser extent, the Carter administration. The Reagan administration's actions to date strongly indicate it shares the perspective of the two previous Republican administrations on this question.

Yet the case of Iran gave additional fuel to critics of the viability of arms sales as an instrument of U.S. foreign policy. In spite of massive transfers to Iran of advanced military equipment, the Iranian government was not immune to revolution from within. With the fall of the Shah in 1979, a critical premise—that security assistance could strongly enhance the prospects for achieving U.S. foreign policy goals—was called into question.

In the early 1980s the security assistance program is once again in a transitional phase. Although historically it has proven in important cases to be a valuable instrument of American foreign policy, it has also failed to ensure outcomes in other important instances where U.S. prestige was clearly placed on the line through its use. In constant dollar terms the grant military aid program and the FMS credit program have not constituted a large portion of the federal budget. The security assistance program nonetheless does not enjoy the broad-gauged support that it did in the 1950s. At a time when policymakers confront critical choices regarding priorities among various domestic programs in the federal budget, the potential benefits of the security assistance program have become harder to communicate to a skeptical audience in both Congress and the nation.

Notes

1. Federal government transfer payments include a comprehensive range of U.S. retirement, social insurance, and welfare benefit payments under various programs. These include Social Security and its various components, state unemployment insurance, workman's compensation, federal government retirement, direct relief, food stamps, and other programs of this nature defined by the National Bureau of Statistics.

2. Data on Defense Department budget authority taken from National Defense Budget Estimates for FY 1982, Office of Comptroller, March 1981, p. 5, and ibid, National Defense Budget Estimates for FY 1983, March 1982, p. 4. MAP program appropriations data taken from Congressional Presentation Document, Security Assistance Programs, FY 1983, DOD, p. 11.

2 Perceptions of U.S. Security Assistance, 1959–1983: The Public Record

Steven A. Hildreth

The Role of Congress in the Security Assistance Process

Although every president since World War II has viewed security assistance[1] as vital to U.S. foreign and defense policy, it has been and remains a beleaguered program. It has become increasingly difficult for each administration to obtain from Congress what it perceives as the requisite level of military aid for the protection of U.S. interests overseas.

To date, however, there have been few efforts to examine the perceptions of security assistance reflected in the public record, specifically in the executive branch, Congress, and the media in a systematic and thorough manner. There is not a clear picture, therefore, of the problems an administration frequently encounters in Congress or faces with the media, which has an indirect impact on this program.

In this chapter the public record of presidential statements, administration presentations, congressional deliberations, and media commentary on the annual security assistance program from 1959 through 1983 are reviewed and appraised.[2] It is therefore important to understand the legislative process.

Each fiscal year the executive submits to Congress its security assistance proposal. Some components of this program involve an annual authorization and appropriation including the Military Assistance Program (MAP),[3] the International Military Education and Training Program (IMET),[4] the Foreign Military Sales Program (FMS credits),[5] the Economic Support Fund (ESF),[6] and Peacekeeping Operations (PKO).[7] Other components, such as foreign military cash sales and commercial exports are also addressed, but from a control, reporting, and oversight perspective, not from a funding standpoint; annual authorization and appropriation are not involved.[8]

Two laws provide the basic framework for the security assistance authorization: (1) the Foreign Assistance Act of 1961, as amended; and (2) the International Security Assistance and Arms Export Control Act of 1976, as amended. The Foreign Assistance Act is the authorizing legislation for most program elements. Most of this act, however, is devoted to programs outside security assistance, such as foreign economic aid, multilateral assistance, the Peace Corps, and the Overseas Private Investment Corporation (OPIC). The other authorizing statute, the Arms Export Control Act (AECA), provides authority for the sale and export of arms, both governmental and commercial. These components were first covered in the Mutual Security Act of 1954, then later in the Foreign Assistance Act of 1961. Foreign military sales were split off in a separate law with the passage of the Foreign Military Sales Act of 1968. The AECA was the next major revision (1976). Besides the permanent authority for foreign governmental and commercial arms sales, this act provides the annual authorization for the FMS credit program through an amendment enacted each year.

Appropriations for security assistance are provided by the Foreign Assistance and Related Programs Appropriations Act, amended annually. If a new fiscal year begins before an appropriation is passed, Congress must pass a "continuing resolution authority" to ensure continued funding levels for existing programs. This is defined as the authority to obligate

> funds against the MAP or IMET appropriation for the new fiscal year under Continuing Resolution Authority granted by Congress in a Joint Resolution making temporary appropriations prior to passage of the regular appropriation act.[9]

Occasionally, specific provisions or amendments in other acts have an impact on security assistance. These will be referred to and discussed later. They too play an important role.

As chief executive, the president is responsible for formulating and presenting the security assistance program and budget to Congress, executing it once it becomes law.

Congress exerts its power in several ways. First, Congress can develop, consider, and act on legislation to establish or amend basic security assistance laws. Second, Congress can appropriate funds for security assistance. Third, Congress can pass joint resolutions in the form of a continuing resolution authority to carry on programs until the regular appropriation process is completed. Fourth, Congress can hold special hearings and investigations, using its own resources such as the General Accounting Office (GAO), the Congressional Research Service (CRS), or the Congressional Budget Office (CBO) to conduct these reviews. Finally, the Senate can ratify treaties having security assistance implications.[10]

Actual work on security assistance legislation is performed by several congressional committees. Since 1974, when the budget committees were established to study the president's budget and recommend changes in fiscal policy and spending priorities (with input from the authorization committees), Congress has been able to analyze the military assistance request and send a budget figure forward for Congress to consider.

Authorization requests are handled largely by the House Committee on Foreign Affairs and the Senate Committee on Foreign Relations, who specify the general aim of the bill and place a ceiling on its funding. Action by the full committee is usually preceded by hearings and recommendations of regional and functional subcommittees.[11] Each committee makes its own recommendations and the bill is presented to the full House or Senate for further debate and voting. The final bill passed in each house is then submitted to a "conference committee," consisting of members of both houses, where major legislative differences are debated in order to produce a final bill amenable to both chambers.[12]

Appropriation bills originate in the House Committee on Appropriations, which may not necessarily approve the amount that was authorized. Normally, these bills are not acted upon until the authorization bill is passed. Both the House and Senate Appropriation Subcommittees on Foreign Operations conduct hearings and recommend bills to the full committees. The floor debate and conference process is similarly repeated. Periodically, however, other bills on special topics related to security assistance are considered by other committees.

The process is essentially one of accommodation, negotiation, and compromise, with special attention paid to majority and ranking members of the committees and subcommittees.

Period I: Cold War Motivations, 1959–1964

With the establishment of the Mutual Defense Assistance Act (1949), the United States defined for itself a major and continuing role in providing materiel and advice to its allies. During the 1950s, with widespread concern over Communist expansion, the United States made a commitment to strengthen governments at the periphery of the Communist bloc by providing military aid. The goal was to create or, at a minimum, preserve stability for governments that allied themselves with the anti-Communist cause.[13]

This rationale was closely linked to the doctrine of containment. Military aid was used to strengthen U.S. and allied capabilities to resist Soviet expansion, and it generally received strong congressional and media support. NATO, SEATO, and nations bordering the Communist world received the most aid.

American politics from 1959 to 1963 continued to produce a relatively strong base of support for military assistance, despite growing opposition from a vocal minority in Congress, particularly over grant aid and arms sales. Instances of fraud, waste, duplicity of aid agencies, and maladministration were cited as the major reasons to revamp the effort.

A variety of other reasons were also used. Labeling it a "give away," opponents reduced grant military aid, with a commensurate increase in loans, thereby placing a portion of the high cost of security assistance on the recipient. Many congressmen also questioned the wisdom of granting military aid to certain developing countries, especially in Latin America; several regimes were cited for abusing military equipment intended for collective security by using such equipment solely for internal security. Consequently, detailed program information was often requested by Congress to better evaluate military aid activities. European allies came under fire for not assuming a fair share of the collective security burden; it was maintained that the United States could no longer afford to shoulder that burden entirely. This perception served to fuel considerable resentment toward the Europeans. Fear that the aid program increased the federal deficit, for example, was also used to legitimize funding reductions. Some congressmen believed that recipient countries had reconverted their aid monies and purchased U.S. gold. During a period when the United States experienced large reductions in gold reserves, this argument became a popular means whereby domestic concerns were given priority over foreign policy considerations.

The executive branch went through the yearly "I'll cut here because I know you overstated the case anyway" game with Congress. It was widely held that the administration requested high funding levels in anticipation of inevitable cuts. Accordingly, Congress implemented reductions without apparent rhyme or reason. On the other hand, it was suggested that the administration padded the budget, fully aware that Congress assumed the above to be correct.

A vicious circle ensued as each branch attempted to second-guess the other each year.

Throughout this period, Presidents Eisenhower, Kennedy, and Johnson sought to rectify these grievances while also shoring up the overall integrity and importance of the program. NATO allies, for example, were encouraged to contribute more to collective security. These presidents also stressed that military aid did not adversely affect the U.S. balance of payments. Moreover, they credited the security assistance program with opening up overseas markets for U.S. investments, thus ensuring a healthy export market and creating domestic jobs. Military aid was also presented to Congress as a low-cost, low-risk political-military response to Soviet overtures in the Third World.

A general political consensus favored military assistance, but this support began to flag after Europe had rebuilt itself with U.S. aid, and particularly after the Cuban missile crisis. A variety of international crises throughout the late 1950s and early 1960s—the Communist takeover in Cuba, the Tokyo riots, the Congolese crisis, the Bay of Pigs invasion, Khrushchev's announced intent to resume nuclear weapons testing during the Berlin Wall crisis (1961) and the erection of the Berlin Wall, and Soviet involvement in Laos—came to an end without direct superpower conflict. In this context, it was a period of relative complacency in which the impetus to counter the Soviet threat began to diminish and with it considerable Cold War rhetoric. Consequently, U.S. security interests were no longer deemed such vital considerations for congressional perusal. Military assistance felt the impact of a brief change in attitude by virtue of a noticeable decrease in funding levels; congressmen turned most of their attention to domestic issues.

Eisenhower and the Draper Committee

During the 1950s, several government studies were undertaken to evaluate the Mutual Security Program.[14] In 1958, President Dwight D. Eisenhower commissioned prominent members of the business and political community to undertake a definitive analysis. The Committee to Study the United States Military Assistance Program (Draper Committee) was assigned the major task of doing "a completely independent, objective, and nonpartisan analysis of the military aspects of [the] Mutual Security Program," and provide recommendations for the "most suitable means whereby the free world's defenses may be insured."[15]

Eisenhower expressed hope that this study, which ran from November 1958 to August 1959, would perform a forthright evaluation of the degree to which military aid could strengthen U.S. allies and friends and advance national security and foreign policy interests. He was particularly interested in the relative emphasis that should be given to military and economic aid programs.

President Eisenhower was strongly supportive of military assistance. As he saw it, the primary purpose of the program was to strengthen the free world against Communist expansion and influence. Military aid was therefore seen as an integral component of foreign policy, playing a vital role in the total U.S. security effort. In 1959 he extolled the program's past accomplishments and criticized its opponents:

> When I hear this program described as a "give away" or "aid to foreigners at the expense of domestic programs," I wonder what sort of America we would have today—whether any funds would be available for any domestic programs—whether all of our substance would not today be devoted to building a fortress America—if we had not had such a program: if the key nations of Europe had been allowed to succumb to communism after the war, if the insurrectionists had been allowed to take over Greece, if Turkey had been left to stand alone before Soviet threats, if Iran had been allowed to collapse, if Vietnam, Laos and Cambodia were now in communist hands; if the Huks had taken control in the Philippines; if the Republic of Korea were now occupied by Communist China. That none of these tragedies occurred, that all of these nations are still among the free, that we are not a beleaguered people is due in substantive measure to the Mutual Security Program.[16]

Such sentiments reflected Eisenhower's campaign to insure adequate funding levels for military assistance.

To no one's surprise, the Draper Committee largely agreed with Eisenhower, and timed the several interim reports to strengthen the president's hand with Congress at key junctures. The first such report stressed the importance of modernizing NATO forces and urged that MAP aid be increased. Eisenhower, however, notified congressional leaders (and made it known publicly) that he would defer any large increase (to go primarily to NATO) until 1960 because of his commitment to a balanced budget for 1959.

The *New York Times* supported these findings, citing the program's crucial need as a relatively inexpensive international security investment.[17] In Boston, the *Christian Science Monitor* noted that though Americans were willing to spend some $40 billion on defense, they begrudged "$4 billion for constructive peaceful purposes."

Moreover, military assistance bought more security for the United States than did the larger defense budget. Similarly, the *Washington Star* assented.[18]

Other newspapers took strong opposing positions. The *Chicago Tribune*, it appeared, took on a personal vendetta. Not only did the editor strongly oppose the program, but the paper commissioned an investigative series for the public to decide "for itself." Using Turkey as a case study, these articles concluded that military aid was worthless.[19] The *Wall Street Journal* urged a reappraisal of what the program could and could not do as an instrument of foreign policy, faulting Eisenhower for his selective use of aid success stories, showing instead where the program had failed to dissuade Communist adventurism. While there was room for some military assistance "the fact is that we can count on our fingers the countries we think could contribute effectively when the troops march."[20] On the West Coast, the *Los Angeles Times* was content to support large program reductions as beneficial to the U.S. taxpayer.[21]

The House Committee on Foreign Affairs released its own interim report evaluating the Mutual Security Program. Military assistance, it found, suffered from a clear case of maladministration. Korea commanded the committee's particular attention due to charges that supplies had been stolen and diverted to civilian use or lost through poor maintenance due to improper controls. Also, many weapon systems were found ill-suited to the security requirements of developing nations whose needs dictated simpler technologies. It concluded that the military assistance effort could and should be improved, authorizing an inspector general and a comptroller post position under the Department of State.[22] This gave Congress authority to deal with DOD more directly on military aid matters, establish financial control, and allow the GAO investigative access to Pentagon records.

Two opposition groups formed in the Senate. One, led by Chairman William Fulbright of the Committee on Foreign Relations, included Senators Hubert Humphrey and John F. Kennedy, and advocated greater emphasis on economic aid. Fulbright maintained,

> my colleagues and I have been concerned that military considerations have played too great a part in the formulation of the program. This is not of course necessarily to say that the amounts requested for military assistance are too large, because weapons are very expensive.[23]

Fulbright became the leading spokesman for reform. In fact, it was his letter to Eisenhower in 1958, signed by seven other committee members, which prompted the Draper study. It was the contention of Fulbright and others that fragile Third World economies could not handle a preponderance of military aid, notably Pakistan and Korea, and the ratio should therefore be balanced in favor of economic aid.

Senator Ellender of the Committee on Appropriations led the second coalition. This group called for major program cuts and was consistently able to reduce the aid budget significantly.

The Draper Committee's third interim report recommended that military aid be included in the DOD budget with a multi-year authorization. The *New York Times* lauded this proposal because it should "put an end to military aid as a football of domestic politics," and later added that one effect of such legislation would be "to bypass a hostile House Appropriations [Foreign Operations] subcommittee headed by Otto Passman."[24] Funding would then be addressed by the Defense Appropriation subcommittee. The administration included military aid in its defense budget for FY 1960, but Passman's subcommittee retained its jurisdiction. Military aid was given a two-year authorization, however, but only on an experimental basis.

The *New York Times* agreed that military assistance "must be continued and better administered, not emasculated or abandoned."[25] It also praised the Draper report for not resolving itself into anti-Communist rhetoric as a premise for foreign aid. The *Washington Post* too noted that despite indications of program mismanagement and fraud, military aid was still necessary. The *Post* was critical, however, of Eisenhower's emphasis on military over economic aid because this threatened to disrupt the congressional consensus over foreign aid; the net reuslt of the Draper report, therefore, would be large overall reductions in military aid.[26]

The final Draper report offered several recommendations that were to have a lasting impact. While constructive criticisms of the administration's program were valuable, the committee concluded, too many criticisms were unjustified "and their wide publication represents a serious handicap to necessary public understanding and acceptance of the program." Therefore, a public relations program should be launched to "inform the American public of the problems and achievements of mutual security and its vital importance to the security of the United States." Furthermore, clear responsibility for military aid should be given to DOD. Similarly, economic aid should be focused in a new Department of State agency. Military aid should not be diminished, especially to those countries "under the gun of Communism," the report urged, adding that "the impression held in some quarters to the effect that our military assistance program is too great in relation to the economic development assistance program is not justified." It was a clear rebuke to Fulbright, Kennedy, and others.

The Draper Committee added it would require more than a military or industrial response to meet the Soviet challenge—it would require "positive individual and national dedication." Such a plea, however, was not well-received everywhere. In Chicago, the *Tribune* opined that this "call to aid was coupled with dedication to work similar to that imposed on the Russian people by their dictators."[27]

On the other hand, the *Chicago-Sun Times* strongly supported the program. "Those who accept the world as it is," wrote the editor, "will accept the principle that this program is as essential a part of our national defense as are ICBMs, Polaris submarines and supersonic bombers for our own military forces." This was the means whereby "free nations" could defend their freedom "against communist subversion."[28] Throughout the 1950s, most newspapers, however, failed to distinguish between the military and economic aid components in their positions toward foreign assistance. One notable exception was the *Christian Science Monitor*, which often reminded the public that military aid was indeed different. To avoid this misperception, both military aid and defense support should be included in the defense budget.[29]

Senator Fulbright and others supported Eisenhower's efforts to concentrate on nonmilitary aid to countries such as India, Pakistan, and Taiwan, while others maintained that domestic considerations should be given priority over foreign policy and, therefore, sought major program reductions. At issue was the outflow of gold and the balance of payments deficit. Some felt that cutting foreign aid would eliminate the balance of payments deficit because it was the one element over which the government exercised considerable control. Fulbright's committee recognized several problems, however. "In assessing this program," it concluded, "one is struck with a paradox. It has been supported strongly since its inception by every president, every Secretary of State, every Secretary of Defense, every Chairman of the Joint Chiefs of Staff, and every Congress." However, "there is unmistakable evidence that the program is misunderstood and disliked by large numbers of the American people" because of faulty program administration, rather than on fundamental policy issues.[30]

These were hot media issues as well. The *Wall Street Journal*, for example, often decried the outflow of gold and the deficit. On one occasion in 1960, after Eisenhower delivered a speech to a pro-aid group (followed by a speech to a second group on strengthening the dollar), the *Journal* cited the incongruity in supporting a program that caused the deficit, yet at the same time advocating a strong dollar position. In Chicago, the *Tribune* similarly attacked Eisenhower's speech and decried aid expenditures in light of a $3 billion deficit.[31]

During the 1960 appropriation process Chairman Passman vowed to slash security assistance by 75 percent. Eisenhower promptly appealed to the public in a nationally televised speech before the Committee for International Economic Growth to halt the actions of certain democrats bent on cutting the aid program; implicit was the reference to Passman: "unless an alert citizenry takes effective action to support those in Congress who champion the cause of mutual security, it could well result in jeopardizing an important part of the nation's defense."[32] Passman skillfully used a series of GAO reports critical of military assistance to convince the Committee on Appropriations to reduce funding levels.[33] (One report singled out a country that had only thirty men qualified to operate tanks, yet was given 350 U.S. tanks—country names remained classified. Another nation had only 186 jet-pilot instructors, yet received 421 jets.) Passman also argued that U.S. allies did not assume an equal share of the defense burden.

Others, however, including Congressman Gerald Ford, were clearly angered by these cuts. They submitted a minority committee report charging, "this is no time to 'kow tow' to Khrushchev or be soft on Communism." They disputed Passman's contention that Europeans were lax in their contributions: "the record shows that whereas the U.S. was paying 28 percent of the total defense costs of our European NATO allies in 1953, we are paying about 8 percent today."[34]

The *Chicago Sun-Times*, an advocate of military assistance, expressed dismay at "a few isolationist die-hards like Rep. Passman . . . [who] can always be depended upon to cry 'give away' to any proposal to cooperate with the allies abroad."[35] Similarly, the *New York Times* labeled these cuts "as potentially dangerous to our foreign policy as it is clearly irresponsible," and the *Los Angeles Times* opposed these cuts because military assistance promoted international and regional stability.[36]

On the eve of Eisenhower's trip to the Near East in 1960 to strengthen alliance relations, he made a last-minute appeal to House members urging them to restore Passman's cuts. The House responded to these pressures and immediately restored half of Passman's cuts in military aid. A coalition of liberals and conservatives had challenged him. Earlier, Passman had reduced funds for the Indus

Basin project (a favorite among Democrats), and the military aid slashes were considered anathema to many Republicans. A pact was reportedly made to ward off cuts in either component when the bill came up for floor consideration.

Despite controversies and setbacks, the military assistance program was generally supported. A few staunch media supporters, however, such as the *New York Times,* began to express concern. After Congress finally passed the 1960 aid bill, the *Times* warned that "it must be hoped that other nations grown prosperous with American aid will now takeup an increasing part of the burden for our common salvation."[37]

The Kennedy Administration

When John F. Kennedy became president in 1961 he argued that the collapse of the "free, but less developed nations" would be disastrous to U.S. security, invite totalitarianism, and endanger Third World stability.[38] Kennedy believed that security assistance was therefore integral to U.S. security, necessary to maintain existing forces, and needed to honor prior commitments.

The 1960 Democratic party platform was a precursor to Kennedy's emphasis favoring economic aid and stressing the need to revamp the entire program.[39] In his initial aid proposal Kennedy criticized Eisenhower's inability to make long-range commitments to developing countries, which he felt enabled the USSR to "advance the aims of world communism"; he also recommended a separate authorization for military aid as part of the defense budget and reprogrammed Eisenhower's proposal to favor economic aid.[40]

His former colleague, Senator Fulbright, praised the new emphasis, while others hoped that program mismanagement would now end. The press also gave praise. Both the *New York Times* and the *Baltimore Sun* urged that MAP be separated and put into the defense budget.[41] The *St. Louis Post-Dispatch* emphasized that because the public did not understand aid this separation would be beneficial and serve to "make clear the peaceful and positive purposes" of aid. Such an effort would prove difficult, however, because legislators are "reluctant to give up their annual authorization authority."[42] The *New York Times* later added that program waste resulted from congressional hamstringing.[43] The *Salt Lake Tribune* expressed hope that U.S. allies would share this burden, but because of the gold crisis, the United States may have reached its limit in "international generosity."[44]

Two months into the Kennedy administration, Vice-President

Lyndon Johnson toured Southeast Asia and reportedly agreed to enlarge the 150,000–man army in South Vietnam by 20,000 and establish an antiguerrilla warfare training program. It was felt that the fall of Laos and South Vietnam would expose all Southeast Asia, and eventually Indonesia, to Communist control.

Kennedy escalated the conflict in Southeast Asia by requesting additional emergency military aid. The *Washington Star* supported this move because it would demonstrate to the Soviet Union U.S. determination to halt Communist aggression. Although the *Salt Lake Tribune* normally was a staunch supporter of military assistance, on this occasion it wrote that "Kennedy's urgency doesn't come through," questioning why the "urgency" for increased aid was any different than earlier in the year.[45]

Again, Passman's subcommittee gutted the military aid proposal out of domestic economic concerns.[46] The *New York Times* urged the full House to restore the cuts: "It is up to Congress as a whole to uphold its word and its honor against the spleen of one of its misguided members."[47] Congressman Gerald Ford quickly restored much of the cuts, and the Senate did likewise. Passman delayed the process until Congress awaited adjournment, and weary of constant bickering, finally reached an agreement in the final days of the session without a formal conference by splitting the difference between himself and his opponents. As passed, the Foreign Assistance Act of 1961 consolidated all previous aid programs and created the Agency for International Development (AID) to administer the nonmilitary programs.[48]

Kennedy returned in 1962 and stressed that military aid was necessary to strengthen the political and economic independence of developing nations by helping them overcome the problems associated with rapid internal change and thus repel Communist efforts to exploit such stress. He emphasized self-help where it was possible, however. To Kennedy, security assistance was a relatively inexpensive and efficient defense instrument.[49]

To ease a major congressional concern, Kennedy assured Congress that U.S. allies had increased their contributions to collective security. Secretary of Defense Robert McNamara told Congress that real reductions could be achieved through tighter controls and country analyses, which could determine military absorptive capacities.

The *Washington Post* and the *Wall Street Journal* criticized Kennedy's 1962 military aid proposal for emphasizing anti-Communist rhetoric: "perhaps, like the Greek general who confessed he could not get his soldiers to fight until he had got them frightened," wrote the *Post*, "foreign aid advocates think Congress will not vote unless it is frightened." According to the *Journal*, this approach was a dangerous misconception. Again, the *Chicago Tribune* opposed aid for domestic reasons, while the *New York Times* remained a supporter.[50]

Kennedy responded to his critics by cautioning them that to

> curtail our foreign aid program in order to strengthen our balance of payments would be to sacrifice more than we gain. A large percentage of our aid is already spent on procurement in the U.S. . . . [and] we will continue our efforts to obtain a higher level of assistance by other industrial nations.[51]

Congress began to exert itself by restricting what the executive could do. For example, when IT&T was expropriated by Brazil in early 1962, Fulbright and others voted to prohibit aid to any country that seized U.S. property. Secretary of State Dean Rusk attempted to thwart Congress' decision because he felt such a law would severely inhibit the execution of the program. The administration won a partial victory when the provision was softened to allow for presidential waiver in cases where U.S. national security interests were considered at stake.[52] Congress also prohibited MAP grants to any country using such aid unlawfully. It also raised concern over the use of U.S. military equipment in unstable Latin American regimes, such as the use of a U.S. Sherman tank that rammed through the gates of the Pizarro Palace in Peru leading a military coup, to which the administration responded by severing all military aid.

The most controversial restriction concerned Cuba. Although military aid to Cuba ended with Fidel Castro's ascension, additional pressure was attempted by cutting off aid to any country that traded with Cuba. Because this would have affected Greece, Italy, and Great Britain, the president was given authority to waive the provision provided he felt it was in the national interest.[53] Congress sent another message to Europe by considering an amendment that would have reduced or terminated aid to any country sufficiently wealthy to procure its own defense items. This theme of terminating aid to those who could provide for their own defense had begun in the late 1950s with aid to Europe.

The House Committee on Foreign Affairs added to Kennedy's problems in 1962 by releasing a report that highlighted waste in the military assistance program.[54] Turkey and South Korea were cited as two of the worst offenders, and were used by Passman as an excuse for large reductions. Averell Harriman, Assistant Secretary of State, warned Congress that if Passman's actions were enacted it "would be the worst setback for the U.S. in 15 years . . . [taking] away our most valuable weapons for winning the Cold War at the same time that we are increasing expenditures for our national defense establishment." Passman and the administration fought bitterly to gain the upper hand throughout 1962.

Kennedy soon began to deal with his opponents more forcefully. "*I am more conscious than ever, sitting where I do,* that we bear

> great responsibilities, and if anyone feels that these countries are unimportant, or that it doesn't make any difference if Latin America is taken over, or significant countries are, by communists; and if they're not interested in this fight then they should cut it.[55]

It was a clear attack against those who consistently mouthed anti-Communist rhetoric, yet ironically advocated large military aid reductions.

Kennedy recognized the increasing difficulty in getting Congress to support his military aid programs and believed that 1963 might prove as frustrating. He therefore commissioned a blue-ribbon panel in late 1962 to review the foreign aid program to determine whether the level and distribution of aid contributed to U.S. security and Third World stability. He hoped this effort would pay off politically and provide him with ammunition to thwart rising (yet still relatively moderate) congressional opposition.

Three months into the new year, the Committee to Strengthen the Security of the Free World chaired by retired general Lucius D. Clay, completed its work.[56] "Dollar for dollar," the committee concluded, these aid programs "contribute more to the security of the free world than corresponding expenditures in our defense appropriations." It suggested that the United States was trying to do too much for too many and that less aid might accomplish more in some countries. The Clay report recommended that NATO should assume a greater defense burden, that military aid should be gradually reduced in cases where it would neither jeopardize nor impair the collective security effort (such as to those nations on the perifery of the Sino–Soviet bloc "with substantial resources of their own," regional powers friendly to the United States that quarelled with another, those who demand excessive assistance for U.S. military base rights), and aid cut to Indonesia because of President Sukarno's human rights abuses and regional adventurism—to which the *Washington Star* believed was one finding that was sure to be "popularly acclaimed."[57]

Most newspapers, however, focused heavily on the recommendations to cut the program. The *Wall Street Journal* stated that

> the U.S. is attempting too much aid for too many and often in the wrong ways; it should curtail the program and pay more attention to its own interests and less to the sensitivities of others. This is about the sum of the thoughtful report to President Kennedy.[58]

The *Washington Post* praised the recommendations to continue military aid to India and Pakistan, but recognized that the Clay report was only going to heat up the debate over the amounts of aid, not the principle of aid. The *New York Times* predicted a "more intense attack than ever as a result of the report," encouraging those "who seek to cut the program." Furthermore, "if the threat of Communism is to be met, this is not the time to be either niggardly or short-sighted." Both the *Christian Science Monitor* and the *Chicago Sun-Times* supported the emphasis, but also added that the recommendations for cuts had been widely misinterpreted.[59]

In the wake of these findings, Kennedy quickly cut his initial request and informed Congress these reflected the Clay report's recommendations. He hoped Congress would be deterred from making further cuts, and argued that military aid procurements contributed favorably to the U.S. economy, and despite

> noisy opposition from the very first days and despite warnings that the Marshall Plan and successor programs were "throwing our money down a rat-hole" . . . the fact is that our aid programs generally and consistently have done what they were expected to do.[60]

Congress was unimpressed, and irrespective of its general support for the report, seized upon and emphasized its anti-aid aspects. In later years, Kennedy's biographer would write:

> With what he [Kennedy] privately acknowledged to be a "calculated risk," he named a panel of conservative private enterprise skeptics to review his 1963 aid request . . . . which recommended cuts while strongly defending the program. Passman and Company ignored the defense, accepted the cuts and made still more cuts—and Kennedy's gamble backfired.[61]

Congress again cut military aid and approved restrictions on phasing out some grant aid to African and Latin American nations, and aid to nations dealing with Communist countries. General Clay made an urgent appeal to 300 of the nation's news editors to rally support for the president, suggesting that Congress had grossly misread his report's conclusions, but it was too little, too late. John F. Kennedy did not live to see the final outcome of this year's debate over military assistance, which ended in the largest reductions in the program's history and the greatest number of congressional restrictions ever.

The Johnson Administration, 1963–1964

President Lyndon B. Johnson did not differ significantly from Kennedy in his views of security assistance. Johnson did, however, intensify his belief that were the United States to default on its global obligations, communism would spread throughout the world. Military assistance was vital because it reduced the dangers and frequency of global crises, was less expensive than regular defense expenditures, served to frustrate the ambitions of Communist imperialism, and supported "the moral commitment of free men everywhere working for a just and peaceful world."

Shortly into 1964, the president made a supplemental aid request for Southeast Asia, which passed amid mounting concern over the region's stability. Johnson was very concerned for those nations "along the periphery of the Sino–Soviet bloc," to which the *Los Angeles Times* replied: it's "too late." In Atlanta, the *Constitution* reaffirmed its support of military aid by asserting that it made no sense at all "to abandon this whole uncertain area [Indochina] to the much more ominous threat of international communism." And the *Wall Street Journal* found Johnson's arguments lacking.[62]

The administration's attitude, as demonstrated during congressional hearings by Secretary of State Dean Rusk, was that aid was necessary to achieve a "safe and stable world," free not only from "20th century Communism," but from the "age-old enemies of man: ignorance, disease and poverty." While some debate took place, no major opposition occurred.[63] The appropriation bill passed with relative ease and marked the first time in a decade that the House had rejected all of Passman's attempts to cut aid. One possible reason may have been that Johnson's long-time friend, Congressman Mahon, had taken over the chairmanship of the full committee (and in 1965 stacked the subcommittee against Passman with pro-aid supporters); the previous chairman had been more willing to go along with Passman. Another reason apparently was the success of Johnson's insistence that the aid budget had not been inflated in anticipation of deep congressional cuts.[64]

Period II: Vietnam and Growing Isolationism, 1965–1975

This period witnessed deep divisiveness in America brought on by the protracted war in Southeast Asia, which impacted directly on the security assistance effort. A fairly common perception of this period was that initial support of the corrupt South Vietnamese regime through military assistance had caused the war to escalate. Not only did a distaste grow for military aid, but also an aversion to foreign involvements in general.

During the initial years, few congressmen raised their voices against increased involvement in Vietnam. Indeed, when President Johnson requested a special supplemental for Vietnam in 1965, the measure passed in lightning speed and only twelve members of Congress dissented.[65] Wayne Morse, a senator vigorously opposed to foreign aid, summed up the sentiments that were to become, in later years, widely held: "I say sadly and solemnly, but out of deep conviction that today my Government stands before the world drunk with military power" and is about to lay the foundation for "intense Asiatic hatred." This resolution, he maintained, gave "the President power to make undeclared war."

The emphasis in U.S. security assistance programs shifted during this ten-year period and reflected the changing international environment. One of the more substantial changes was greater emphasis on military aid to developing countries because Western Europe had become more self-sufficient. Anticommunism still drove the program, however, even though it was less explicit under Richard Nixon. The major program cost shifted from Europe to Asia. The 1967 Arab–Israeli War, however, set the stage and ushered in a new era of substantial aid funds to the Middle East—one that today dominates and demands the greatest share of the security assistance budget.

With each passing year, Congress became increasingly assertive in foreign policy, and opposed to security assistance. To be sure, this phenomenon was rooted largely in the Vietnam conflict. As successive administrations were drawn into the war, and later into Cambodia, Congress learned the art of legislative guerrilla warfare. Watergate was an additional catalyst and journalists throughout the nation encouraged Congress to take the reins of government and lead the country out of the proverbial abyss. Détente caused the public to focus less on foreign problems. Various studies of economic and security assistance were proferred by the executive branch, but mostly fell on deaf congressional ears. Congress was quick to absorb many of the powers that eroded in the executive branch during this period, especially in foreign policy.

As mentioned earlier, the latter end of this period witnessed a significant shift in aid to the Middle East, primarily arms sales. In part this grew out of the perennial Arab–Israeli conflict and the surge in oil prices that enabled oil-exporting countries to purchase arms on a large scale. The shift in arms transfer policy from grants to sales was more acceptable to Congress and was also a direct consequence of the Nixon Doctrine (and Vietnam)—the United States would assist its friends and allies, but they would be responsible for protecting themselves to reduce the U.S. presence overseas.

However, the issue of U.S. arms transfer policies and congressional concern over human rights violations quickly grew to dominate the legislative debates in the mid- to late-1960s, and particularly after 1973. Middle Eastern instability, the Indo–Pakistani and Bangladeshi Wars, and a series of political mishaps in Latin America served to fuel congressional resolve for tighter control over the sale of commercial and government-supplied arms.

This shift also reflected a change from the explicit emphasis on anticommunism and the consequent benefits to the United States derived from reliance upon anti-Communist regional powers. The thrust now became one of enhancing U.S. ability to influence others and pursue U.S. foreign policy objectives.

The Johnson Administration, 1965–1968

In his 1965 State of the Union Address, President Johnson reconfirmed his support of U.S. involvement in Vietnam, emphasizing that he would not break the pledge made by three previous presidents to assist the South Vietnamese people in resisting Communist aggression. Although there were few opponents of this strategy, a chorus of opposition had begun to grow in the media and in Congress. "What is clearly open to question," wrote the *New York Times* after his speech, "is whether the method chosen is the one the United States or the South Vietnamese are capable of implementing successfully."[66] The *New York Times* later faulted this "policy of drift" in Indochina, which was getting "more and more dangerous, carrying with it, as it does, the possibility of falling by inadvertence and indirection into a major war." The *Times* also opposed U.S. involvement in African political turmoil through military aid.[67]

Johnson continued to emphasize that security assistance was needed to meet the challenge of communism and match the Soviet's expanding aid program. Military assistance made it possible for nations to survive, providing a shield behind which social and economic development could occur, and was a low-cost deterrent to Chinese and Soviet aggression. Johnson recognized, however, that it was a limited policy instrument and certainly no cure-all for every national security problem the United States faced.[68]

In May 1965, a significant vote took place when Congress voted unanimously for a bill allowing FY 1965 supplemental appropriations of $700 million for U.S. military operations in Vietnam. The approval came less than two days after Johnson appealed to Congress to show "prompt support of our basic course: resistance to aggression, moderation in the use of power, and a constant search for peace." This marked the first time that the administration asked specifically for a defense appropriation for Vietnam, as an addition to the regular military budget.[69]

The *New York Times* called this move a "vote of confidence" for Johnson who could easily have obtained the money "by transferring funds within the Defense Department." The *Times* believed, however, that Congress had lost control over foreign policy by allowing Johnson to rush the bill through so quickly without formal hearings.[70] But the *Wall Street Journal* argued that the request and quick response indicated that Johnson would not retreat from Southeast Asia.[71] Most, however, paid scant attention to the story because of the invasion of the Dominican Republic by U.S. Marines.

Later in the year, the administration returned to Congress for approval of an additional $1.7 billion for Vietnam in the FY 1966 defense budget. These requests constituted the beginning of the Military Assistance Service Fund (MASF) program—an effort designed to circumvent the regular military aid authority process by avoiding the Senate Committee on Foreign Relations, which had grown increasingly hostile to the war in Asia.

Johnson saw his "Vietnam Supplemental" as a vote "to persist in our efforts to halt Communist aggression in South Vietnam," suggesting that each congressman who supported it was saying that the "Congress and the President stand united before the world in joint determination that the independence of South Vietnam shall be preserved and Communist attack will not succeed."[72] Others saw it differently, and a vocal minority refused to consider the bill a "blank check" in support of the administration's Vietnam policy.

In 1966, President Johnson reaffirmed that security assistance should be given only to nations that were not hostile to the United States and were determined to help themselves, a point President Kennedy had made years earlier. Johnson stressed that this strategy helped avert wars and crises. He then proposed that economic and military assistance be handled in separate legislation and each given a five-year authorization in order to clarify "the goals and functions of these programs in the minds of the public and the Congress," "signify the depth" of U.S. commitments, and "free Congress from the burden of an annual renewal of basic legislation."[73]

This move was hailed by the *New York Times*, even though it was "a belated if indirect tribute to the wisdom of [Fulbright]."[74] Similarly, the *Christian Science Monitor* said these steps would lead to greater efficiency, while the *Wall Street Journal* and the *Chicago Tribune* continued to decry the adverse domestic economic consequences of all aid.[75]

Secretary McNamara argued before Congress that shifting the South Vietnamese military aid program to the Defense Department would ensure greater military efficiency in that country. He cautioned that other developments in Southeast Asia, however, particularly the "threat of Communism" in Thailand and Laos, could further raise the costs of military aid.[76]

In 1965, for the first time, Senator Fulbright almost refused to be the floor manager of the aid bill, a result of his growing opposition to its emphasis on military aid (indeed there were Senate calls in 1965 to end military aid by 1967, but the House balked), and the Vietnam War. Fulbright again led the opposition in 1966 criticizing the aid program, particularly bilateral aid because it was seen as a factor in committing the United States to foreign interventions, and in Vietnam. The Senate Committee on Foreign Relations reported that consideration of the aid bill was "inevitably influenced by the war in Vietnam," noting that many in Congress felt that the United States was either "overcommitted, or in danger of being overcommitted, in the world at large." Also, "considerable uneasiness over the military program in its present form," was expressed, especially in that grant aid as well as sales had been

> too readily furnished to too many countries which [could not]—[nor] should not—support sizable military establishments and which [were] too often more interested in using arms against each other than against a common foe—this aid should emphasize civic action programs.[77]

Meanwhile, the House Committee on Foreign Affairs urged Congress not to dictate its Vietnam dissatisfaction by cutting aid or "by establishing arbitrary limitations" on countries receiving aid, because such actions were ineffective in directing U.S. foreign policy.[78] Nationally, the media too was sharply divided over Fulbright's criticism of the war. While many backed the administration, others supported a growing minority who opposed increasing U.S. aid. Few remained neutral.

For the balance of the year there were continued Senate concerns over abuses of military aid and arms sales (such as those involved in the Indo–Pakistani War, the 1967 Arab–Israeli War, and the military coup in Argentina),[79] but the House did not always agree. Nonetheless, some restrictions resulted, which Johnson called "unduly and unnecessarily limiting."

In a speech not delivered on the floor, but later inserted in the *Congressional Record,* Senator Thomas Dodd argued that the most damaging factor responsible for the major aid setbacks "was the full-fledged emergence in this year's debate of a neo-isolationism which threatens the entire structure of our foreign policy." Whatever their motivations, "it is difficult to escape the impression that they are using the foreign aid program . . . as an instrument of [political] pressure in an effort to compel the Administration to revise its Vietnam policy."[80]

President Johnson counterattacked in 1967, indicating that the threat to U.S. security posed by internal subversion and insurgency could not be countered by U.S. withdrawal, isolation, or indifference.[81] Security assistance should be used to strengthen countries on the periphery of China and Russia to thwart Communist expansion. This he felt would reduce the chances of future Vietnams, but added this would take a long time. Johnson reiterated that the primary goal of the program was to create a community of independent and prosperous nations that would then serve as the best long-term guarantee of a "secure America in a peaceful world"—the way to global peace.

The *New York Times* reaffirmed its support of economic and military aid as a "moral obligation that goes with worldwide power and responsibility," expressing concern that "Washington should be exploring ways to stretch aid rather than shrink it."[82]

Congress, however, handed Johnson a major defeat, cutting aid to its lowest level ever (Johnson lamented that this had reduced "the margin of hope to the danger point"). Congress also refused to grant an advance authorization sought for the program for FY 1969 (it even withdrew FY 1969 authorizations that had already been tentatively approved in 1966). In addition, Congress again restricted the executive. It ended DOD's authority to finance credit sales to developing countries, required that aid be terminated to nations whose defense spending interfered "materially" with their growth, and required the executive to furnish it with greater detail about projected aid commitments.

The *New York Times* felt that Johnson accepted these restrictions too easily, suggesting that he was perhaps hoping to gain certain concessions. Such political jockeying, the *Times* believed, was not demonstrative of good presidential leadership.[83]

Most opposition in 1967 focused on two major factors. First, there was growing congressional discontent (principally in the Senate), over the direction of U.S. foreign policy and lack of congressional consultation, particularly regarding Vietnam. Second, there was overwhelming congressional concern (principally in the House), over cost reductions because of a growing budget deficit, continued high levels of war spending, and the resulting threat of inflation.[84]

Another major source of controversy was the Pentagon's revolving fund for financing arms sales, which, until 1967, was not widely known, even in Congress. Earlier, Senator Eugene McCarthy released a study by the Committee on Foreign Relations accusing the Pentagon of contravening U.S. foreign policy objectives, particularly in arms control, by "aggressive" arms sales promotion.[85] And the *New York Times* ran a series on the arms sales business, which cast a negative light on the U.S. role. The paper suggested that a reason why foreign aid encountered so much opposition was its lack of a constituency, and that it remained "the most sensitive lightning rod for all of the House's frustrations and resentments" in dealing with the president.[86] Once publicized, the Senate voted to end the program, but the House favored its continuation. Critics were concerned that this program was a "back-door" method of arms financing, accelerated the arms race (for example, in the Middle East), diverted scarce resources for economic development, and engaged the United States unnecessarily in foreign conflicts (that is, Vietnam).

The administration countered that these arms transactions were necessary to regional stability and to prevent these countries from relying upon the Communist bloc for military aid. A policy paper from the Departments of State and Defense informed Capitol Hill that moves to curb such sales would wreck the alliance and unilaterally disarm friendly Third World states. An extended deadlock deferred the decision until 1968. Congress did stipulate that no defense article or service could be provided unless the president found that the transaction would strengthen U.S. security and promote world peace, and the recipient country agreed not to transfer those articles to a third country without the consent of the president (who had to inform Congress).

Johnson's FY 1969 aid request was the smallest ever, and was different from others in that it did not propose to extend the administration's authority to sell military equipment on credit. Because this had been so controversial, Johnson presented it in separate legislation. Also, for the first time (because of congressional pressure), the proposed funding levels for military aid were submitted on an unclassified basis for public scrutiny, although hearings remained closed.

The difficulties that lay ahead were predicted by the media. The *Washington Post,* for example, wrote: "foreign aid is in a terrible fix this year. Vietnam has given all foreign involvement a sour taste." Moreover, this small request suggests that Johnson wants to put the program on temporary hold "to buy time until Congress will accept the kind of sweeping program that American interests require."[87]

As things heated up, Secretary McNamara, according to the *Wall Street Journal,* challenged Congress to decide once and for all whether it still believed "in the collective defense of the free world and [was] willing to pay the cost, or whether it wishe[d] the U.S. to return to isolationism."[88] Secretary Rusk stressed that U.S. national interests were directly tied to Third World development. Military aid therefore served

1. to strengthen the capability of selected allied and friendly nations against the threat of external attack and
2. help developing nations protect their societies against internal violence, thus providing the framework of stability within which national development [could] thrive.[89]

Many House Republicans decried the aid program and scored India for criticizing the United States while being the largest single aid recipient (1968) and diverting scarce resources to purchase sophisticated arms and build weapon plants. In the Senate, Secretary Rusk finally appeared before the Committee on Foreign Relations after considerable controversy and complaints that he appear and answer for Vietnam to, according to the *Washington Star,* "present himself for public flagellation."[90] Fulbright demanded that the hearings focus on Vietnam because it was "not possible to talk about foreign aid, or indeed any problem of this country's foreign relations, without discussing the war." Several senators used the media event to voice anti-war sentiments.[91] The *New York Times* expressed hope that Rusk's argument—that the United States could not find security and peace apart from the rest of the world—would be heeded by Congress. Rusk's answers on Vietnam, however, "the issue uppermost in the minds of the Senate and foremost in the thought of the nation," sounded "as has been observed before, like a broken record. . . . his testimony implies a readiness to escalate the American military effort still further."[92]

Because the administration proposed a separate military sales request, Clark Clifford, the new Secretary of Defense, said this would be limited to grant aid, most of it going to Greece, Turkey, Iran, South Korea, and Taiwan. "The primary role of military assistance," he said, "has been—and continues to be—to supply arms, equipment and training to fill the gap between what our allies need for deterrence and what their economies can provide."[93] As passed, the Foreign Military Sales Act of 1968 authorized DOD to guarantee the credit of less-developed countries wishing to purchase U.S. arms as an alternative to the department's "Country X revolving fund" that provided credit (or backed Ex-Im Bank credit) on arms sales, which Congress had just terminated. All funds for credit sales would come from obligational authority provided annually by Congress, and under the State Department, "consistent with our foreign policy objectives."[94] Congress further prohibited MAP funds from being used to furnish modern weapons to others, unless the president deemed it vital to national security, and urged that military training programs be reviewed. Finally, a large arms sales agreement was made with Israel because of its losses in the 1967 war.

The Nixon Administration: A "New Foreign Policy for the 1970s"

When Richard M. Nixon became president he set out to "reorganize and revitalize" the foreign aid program. Earlier, the president-elect had heard the results of the "President's General Advisory Committee on Foreign Assistance Programs (the Perkins Committee)," which concluded that military aid did not lead to "dangerous military entanglements." The committee urged Nixon to build public and congressional support for aid, and urged Congress to separate military and economic aid and transfer the former to the defense budget (as with similar attempts in the past, this too went nowhere).[95]

Nixon firmly believed that international security problems required military strength sufficient to deter aggression; security assistance played a critical role in that formulation. He believed, however, as the Nixon Doctrine suggested, that other nations should assume the burden of their own defense as much as possible in order to reduce the U.S. presence abroad.[96]

While Congress generally lauded this emphasis it continued to cut aid as part of a more general anti-inflationary budget reduction effort. Congress also remained unconvinced that U.S. military aid commitments did not lead to foreign interventions. Other congressional concerns in 1969 focused on Soviet aid to India and Pakistan (U.S. policy restraint in providing arms to South Asia was perceived as a failure), basing rights to Spain and Thailand (this resulted in major strains in congressional-executive relations), aid to the Greek and South Korean military regimes, and the diversion of scarce resources in developing nations to purchase modern weapon systems. The most controversial issue was aid to Taiwan for modernizing its air force. Neither the House nor the Senate could find agreement, and the administration's position was unclear. This resulted in the failure (for the first time) to complete an appropriation bill before Congress adjourned.[97] When it returned in 1970, Congress agreed to eliminate earmarked funds for Taiwan.

President Nixon formed a second foreign aid commission, which completed its work in 1970. The Peterson Report recommended again that all types of security assistance (military aid and sales, supporting assistance, and the contingency fund) be combined into one act, separate from the economic program, with the Department of State exercising "firm policy guidance" over the military programs. It also proposed ending grant aid and gradually replacing it with credits.[98] Nixon's aid proposal to Congress paralleled these recommendations and were framed within his broader approach to foreign policy—the Nixon Doctrine. Later in the year, the president made a supplemental aid request for Israel ($500 million to purchase military equipment), for his Vietnamization effort ($65 million, mostly for economic aid grants), and military aid grants for Cambodia, Indonesia, Taiwan, South Korea, Jordan, Lebanon, Greece, and Turkey ($340 million).

In response, the *Wall Street Journal* agreed that aid expenditures for political or military purposes should be separated from economic assistance.[99] The *New York Times* also agreed with "such long-overdue reforms."[100] In Chicago, however, responding to Nixon's reference to his committee's recommendations as "fresh and exciting," the *Tribune* wrote, "this is like saying that turkey tetrazzini a week after Thanksgiving is a fresh taste sensation."[101]

Congress continued to assert itself in U.S. foreign policy through the security assistance program. Military training programs were carefully scrutinized by the House Subcommittee on National Security Policy and Scientific Developments (but no action was taken), executive prerogatives with regard to foreign military sales were further curtailed, restrictions on aid to Communist countries and to nations trading with Cuba or North Vietnam were eliminated, and the Cooper–Church Amendment (which failed) would have barred funds for future U.S. military involvement in Cambodia; it was the most significant attempt by Congress to use its powers to conduct U.S. foreign policy.

The media, however, who had generally grown antagonistic toward Vietnamization, used the Cooper–Church initiative to lambast the administration. The *San Francisco Chronicle* wrote that to deny the president funds in this venture would reinforce the view that already existed in Congress that Congress was strongly opposed to the expansion of the war in Southeast Asia. Similarly, the *Pittsburgh Post-Gazette* indicated that the Senate was "properly seeking to regain congressional war-making authority," to which Nixon "would be wise to heed."[102] In Washington, the *Post* agreed that if Nixon continued to escalate the war then the Cooper–Church amendment should be passed "to restore some measure of congressional influence over events."[103]

Nixon took the offensive in 1971 to shore up his faltering security assistance effort. He reaffirmed that security assistance strengthened the defense capabilities and economies of friends and allies, reduced the direct military presence of the United States abroad (and the future likelihood of direct U.S. involvement), supported efforts of countries moving toward economic growth and social progress, and (its primary purpose) preserved peace through deterring war. Nixon also stressed the primacy of allied cooperation in this effort. Even though the program was unpopular, he argued that its role in maintaining national security was indispensible.[104]

For the first time, however, Congress refused to approve a foreign aid bill. The defeat resulted from Senate conservatives (who argued that despite the amount of money given out, the United States failed to gain international support for its policies) and liberals (who contended that aid had been taken over by excessive military concerns, was ineffective in its humanitarian efforts, and should be funneled through international institutions), many of whom had previously been pro-aid.[105]

One contributing factor to such opposition was the disclosure that Food for Peace funds were being used to purchase weapons, to which the *New York Times* commented: "this procedure is only one in a bizarre assortment that add up to the fact that no one in Washington really knows how much the United States spends on military aid to other countries." Congress must take a more active role in monitoring "all aspects of military assistance and to assess its effectiveness."[106] The *Denver Post* added that "using subterfuge for foreign military aid, as in the case of the Food for Peace program, can only serve to discredit all military assistance—the proper as well as the improper."[107]

The White House reacted to this defeat tersely:

> President Nixon feels this vote by the Senate is a highly irresponsible action which undoes 25 years of constructive bipartisan foreign policy and produces unacceptable risks to the national security. . . . It is up to the Congress to act immediately to restore a coordinated foreign aid program . . . a piecemeal or patchwork restoration . . . is not an alternative.[108]

This encouraged the media. The *Boston Globe* suggested that Nixon's assistance to authoritarian regimes had "sparked the tempers of liberal senators . . . and resulted in the coalition of normally pro-aid liberals and anti-aid conservatives who killed the whole package."[109] The *New York Times* went so far as to urge "that a new foreign aid concept [was] required."[110]

Not everyone praised Congress, however. The *Wall Street Journal* wrote it would "be far from easy to undo the grave doubts this capricious action raises about Congress' ability to play a constructive role in foreign affairs." This decision was "not the product of any consistent rationale, but of the chance consequences of varied and often inconsistent elements."[111]

Congressional liberals and conservatives and the executive branch continued to become polarized as global events exacerbated their differences. For example, the Bangladesh crisis, overwhelming UN support for admission of the PRC (and Taiwan's consequent expulsion), U.S. support of the Greek military, and the continuing war in Southeast Asia, especially in Cambodia, were used by aid opponents of differing ideologies as reasons for cutting off all assistance. The Senate, in particular, had now become openly hostile to Nixon's Vietnamization program.

It was well into 1972 before the FY 1972 aid bill passed, ending a long congressional struggle. A compromise was eventually reached, but only after various oblique amendments were rejected. Congress did place a ceiling on the amount of aid to Cambodia (excluding some funds for South Vietnamese operations in Cambodia), limited the number of U.S. personnel and third-country nationals paid by the United States stationed in Cambodia, transferred military aid authorizations for Thailand from the Pentagon to the foreign aid budget (giving the two foreign affairs committees effective control), limited presidential authority in transferring military and security supporting assistance from one nation to another, and required periodic authorization of State Department and USIA appropriations (giving the two foreign affairs committees jurisdiction over these funds too).

The FY 1973 foreign aid bill, however, died in conference, marking the third time in four years that Congress failed to complete action before the year ended. The major disagreement revolved around two Senate initiatives. One would have cut off funds to implement a 1971 executive agreement with Portugal for an air base in the Azores unless the agreement was approved by the Senate as a treaty. The other would have barred the use of funds to carry out any future agreement for military base rights, again unless it was ratified as a treaty.

To many, the belief that Vietnam had indeed overtaken the aid program was already an accepted fact. The *Baltimore Sun*, for example, noted that congressional willingness to assert itself against the executive branch demonstrated deep congressional opposition to U.S. involvement in Southeast Asia.[112]

Many were divided over Congress' proper role (and means) to end the Vietnam War. Although it could sympathize with various Senate amendments to the aid bill to bring an end to the war, the *Washington Post* added that this "could undercut the President's strategy [and] would not bring about an end to the war." Furthermore, we "doubt the wisdom, and still more the practical purpose" of such moves.[113] On the other hand, the *New York Times* believed these Senate "end-the-war resolutions" were, in fact, nothing more than

> Nixon's own Vietnamization program carried to its logical—and long overdue—conclusion. Their adoption and their acceptance by the President could unite the country for peace.[114]

As the result of a major policy shift, the largest foreign aid bill since 1953 was passed in late 1973. Congressional sponsors were quick to note that Nixon's emergency aid requests, primarily to Cambodia and Israel (the 1973 Yom Kippur War had caused Israel to purchase $1 billion in U.S. military equipment in a two-week period with U.S. financial help), were the primary causes behind the increase. It marked the first time that Israel was given grant military aid.[115] Previously, such aid had been in the form of cash sales and credit purchases.

Earlier in the year, considerable controversy was sparked when the administration proposed to sell jet fighters to several Arab and Latin states. "The new trend in arms sales," wrote the *Christian Science Monitor*, "is reminiscent of Charles de Gaulle's methods in boosting the sales of French weapons wherever he could find a market. Unfortunately, such methods will only encourage the arms race around the world."[116] Across town, the *Boston Globe* added that the idea of providing weapons to areas

> notoriously unstable and given to international feuding is mad enough. But the willingness to set up an American presence that could trap us as we were trapped in Vietnam seems the height of lunacy.[117]

The *Washington Post* expressed weariness of this overused rationale, that if the United States ever conducted an arms transaction "it did not try to justify in terms of supposed enhancement of 'stability', it is not on the record. But using the word does not make it so."[118] To the administration's defense came the *Los Angeles Times:*

> The real threat, to their [Saudi and Kuwaiti] national interests, however, does not come from Israel but from neighboring militant Arabs. They know it, and the United States knows it, which is why the Persian Gulf arms deal makes sense.[119]

Nixon suffered his biggest defeat this year, however, when Congress overrode his veto of the War Powers Resolution, which restricted the executive's war-making powers, and reflected congressional impatience for a greater foreign policy role. Nixon branded the bill as dangerous and unconstitutional.

President Nixon launched another concerted effort to sell security assistance to an antagonistic Congress in 1974. He stressed that such an aid program was necessary to build a lasting structure for world peace and development, represented one of the most useful tools for shaping peaceful relationships in the most turbulent areas of the world, designed to create a global environment in which tolerance and negotiation could replace aggression and subversion as preferred methods of conflict resolution, and strengthened the economies of recipients.[120] Nixon made major aid requests for the Middle East (after the 1974 cease fire) and for reconstruction in Southeast Asia. His concerns were soon overshadowed, however, by the Watergate scandal.

The Ford Administration, 1974

Turkey's invasion of Cyprus in July 1974, ostensibly designed to protect Cyprus's ethnic minority from the Greek Cypriot majority, resulted in an arms embargo against Turkey. While analysts have argued that the embargo reflected the emergence of an influential pro-Greek lobby, others believe that important congressional consideration was given to U.S. law that required cutting off military aid to countries using U.S. weapons for other than defensive purposes. The Ford administration's rationale was that greater national interests were at stake.[121] But another factor was important—the overall atmosphere in congressional-executive relations because of Vietnam and congressional desires to curtail executive foreign policy.

Ultimately, it took Kissinger's personal lobbying to get proponents of an immediate cutoff of military aid to Turkey to delay it temporarily until early 1975. While the *Washington Post* saw this extension as a "definite gamble," the *Wall Street Journal* felt that little would be gained by alienating Turkey.[122]

President Gerald Ford tried to bring order to a nation in chaos and repair the government after Nixon's fall, but Congress and the public gave him little room. Ford believed strongly about what security assistance could do for regional stability and peace, but Congress continued its efforts to terminate the military assistance program.

A Senate Committee on Foreign Relations report concluded

> at present the far-flung network of U.S. military missions and military groups gives bureaucratic momentum to the perpetuation of an extensive program the rationale for which each year has become increasingly dubious . . . the program not only escalates the destructive potential of international conflict but also enhances the relative power of the military within these societies and thereby creates undesirable tendencies away from the very democratic processes which the program . . . was intended to defend.[123]

The committee's deep cut for grant assistance was an attempt to initiate this phaseout. U.S. security assistance would still continue, but through foreign military sales, credits, and guarantees. The committee tried to return U.S. arms transactions to commercial channels and thus minimize the government's role in arms sales negotiations, and barred the government from selling any defense article to an "economically developed" country if that article were available through commercial U.S. channels (this provision would not apply to Israel, however). The question of arms sales dominated the committee's concerns, which declared "very strongly that U.S. policies should be geared to restricting, not expanding, the world arms trade." Furthermore,

> out of one side of the government's mouth come pious calls for action to reduce the world's arms burden. And out of the other side comes an arms sales pitch to nations around the globe. The committee hopes that the provision recommended will be a significant step toward ending this hypocritical situation.[124]

Congress then adopted two important amendments. One cut off all security assistance to the post-Allende regime in Chile in an effort to exert U.S. influence and improve human rights conditions there. Congress also approved a Senate amendment (the Nelson amendment), giving itself a legislative veto power over foreign military sales decisions.

The House tried to increase Congress' oversight role by placing limits on the president's discretionary authority and imposed aid ceilings on several countries, earmarked portions for specific countries, restricted the transfer of funds from one program to another, and limited overseas CIA activities.

On the key issue of the future of military aid, House and Senate conferees backed away from the Senate-backed provision requiring termination of the military aid program by the end of FY 1976. Instead, they agreed to express the "sense of Congress" that the program be reexamined and terminated as quickly as was compatible with U.S. foreign policy and national security interests. Congress then directed that the president provide it within one year a detailed plan for the program's eventual elimination.

Period III: Human Rights, Arms Sales, and a "New Beginning," 1975–1983

During this period, support for security assistance waned. The trend toward congressional assertion, inaugurated in previous years, intensified and became a powerful force that the executive branch could no longer stop. For most of these years, Congress repeatedly failed to complete action on either the authorization or appropriation bills. Instead, emergency funding measures in the form of a continuing resolution became accepted practice.

Human rights and arms transfer issues embroiled Congress in heated debate. As a consequence, several major pieces of legislation were passed including the Arms Export Control Act (AECA), which placed stringent control over the execution of U.S. arms transfer policy. Supporters of this legislation noted that military grants were often directed to nations and regions where potential conflict was relatively high. This type of aid, it was argued, exacerbated the situation and led to incidents of aggression. Sometimes this occurred between nations that the United States had armed or supported. Furthermore, because political instability was generally high in the Third World, the neighbors of states backed with U.S. arms often turned to the Soviet Union for assistance. This further strained U.S.–Soviet relations and raised the potential for U.S.–Soviet confrontation. Criticism was voiced over whether such aid was useful, if not detrimental, to long-term U.S. interests. In several cases, the infusion of massive amounts of sophisticated weaponry was incapable of thwarting internal instability (for example, the rise of the Ayatollah Khomeini in Iran).

Into this context a populist new president entered, who asked while campaigning: "can we be both the world's leading champion of peace and the world's leading supplier of the weapons of war?" After taking office, President Jimmy Carter announced that arms transfers would be viewed as "an exceptional foreign policy implement, to be used only in instances where it can be clearly demonstrated that the transfer contributes to our national security." His policy of "restraint" was plagued with problems, however. For one, it resulted in a net increase in arms sales. Secondly, his policy of "flexibility" on human rights and security assistance soon caused Congress to turn on him. Near the end of his term his policies had virtually no political support.

On the other hand, the Reagan administration, backed by what it perceived as a "mandate for change" has abandoned all restraint and set out to arm the Third World, to which it has succeeded.[125] The use of military aid to achieve U.S. diplomatic goals has become a key element of U.S. policy. Furthermore, there now appear the beginnings of a shift away from loans back to grants.

The Ford Administration, 1975–1976

In the aftermath of Watergate, President Gerald Ford appealed to Congress for a "nonpartisan foreign policy." While those such as the *Birmingham News* felt this "should not go unheeded," others like the *Philadelphia Inquirer* reaffirmed that

> Congress has a legitimate role to play in formulating our foreign policy. "Responsible conduct" does not oblige Congress as a whole or any Congressman to surrender their convctions about what is best for America.[126]

In Salt Lake City, the *Tribune* added that the U.S. Constitution made

> the people the third party in "shaping all broad matters of public policy, both foreign and domestic." Congress knows this. It is time the White House learn it. Or more properly, remember it.[127]

The acrimonious atmosphere across the country brought on by the divisive war in Vietnam, the virtual foreign policy monopoly under Kissinger, and the spectre of Nixon's Watergate were still very evident in the media, the Congress, and in the eyes of a skeptical public.

Ford continued to have problems over the Turkish arms embargo, arguing that Turkish aid was neither based in the context of Cyprus, nor as a favor granted to Turkey. Rather, military aid was based on common conclusions that Turkey's security was vital to the security of the eastern Mediterranean and ultimately to that of the United States and its allies.[128] Later, Ford added that his basic approach to security assistance was to give material support to friends and allies willing and able to carry out the burden of their own self-defense—a clear reaffirmation of the Nixon Doctrine.[129]

But many sided with Congress when Turkish aid was finally suspended. The *Washington Post* quite confidently responded, "we think no self-respecting Congress could have acted differently." Furthermore, the Ford Administration needed to swallow its

> anger and apprehension and treat Congress with reasonable respect . . . otherwise the Administration risks shredding its basis for expecting responsible congressional participation in making foreign policy, and exacerbating the very real political tensions that it is in the nation's *real* interest to ease.[130]

Going even further, the *Seattle Times* predicted that other countries, including the United States' closest allies, would just have to get accustomed to Congress taking a firmer hand than it had in the past in conducting U.S. foreign policy.[131]

Congress' decision during the winter of 1975–1976 to cut off funds "for any activities involving Angola directly or indirectly" was similar to the Turkish case. Both Ford and Kissinger had sought to retain a degree of latitude and flexibility traditionally given the executive branch on foreign policy matters, but at one point President Ford lamented:

> How can the United States, the greatest power in the world, take the position that the Soviet Union can operate with impunity many thousands of miles away with Cuban troops and massive amounts of military equipment, while we refuse any assistance to the majority of the local people who ask only for military equipment to defend themselves?[132]

The *Washington Post* quickly responded, declaring that the administration's insistence on compounding the error of its

> Angolan ways is downright masochistic. . . . In post-Vietnam post-Watergate Washington, the Executive does not have such political resources. Accordingly, it must be selective when it undertakes to use or sponsor force abroad.[133]

And in Rhode Island, the *Providence Journal* exclaimed: "What Americans are witnessing in a drawn-out debate over Angola is an unsettling confusion over this country's global means, ends, tactics, purposes and that indefinable quality called our national will."[134]

In the early 1970s there was a sense of unease, both in the media and in Congress, over excesses in U.S. arms sales. Some of this was concern over quantitative excesses (such as in the Persian Gulf), while some was over qualitative excesses (that is, transfers of the most modern weapons). Furthermore, there were numerous revelations, disclosures, and congressional hearings that focused on the role of U.S. business in arms sales, and mostly on instances of bribery and corruption and what appeared to be an uncontrolled "pushing" of U.S. arms abroad without adequate restraints based on foreign policy objectives.[135] The debate over arms sales dominated much of 1976.

For the first time, Congress separated foreign military assistance and sales programs from economic development aid at the authorization stage. According to a report from the Senate Committee on Foreign Relations, this was done to revise long-disputed statutes governing grants and sales of military equipment. Congress then gave itself authority to control sales of major military weapons and equipment. Specifically, Congress was allowed thirty days in which it could veto most arms sales contracts, and imposed a $9 billion a year ceiling on total arms sales. Ford labeled these initiatives an infringement on his constitutional responsibilities, and vetoed the bill. Congress did not have the two-thirds vote to override his veto, and the initiatives were, for the most part, dropped.

Since 1954 military sales through commercial channels had been governed by the Mutual Security Act, a provision of which allowed the president complete control over the program. The above-mentioned report noted this was "an anachronism of an era when Congress chose to leave major foreign policy matters to the president." Perhaps foreshadowing the 1976 initiatives was an amendment to the FY 1975 aid bill that imposed a $25 million ceiling on the sale of military equipment abroad and a requirement that the government notify Congress of government-to-government sales. Prior to passage of this measure, such sales were authorized by the Foreign Military Sales Act of 1971. Efforts to strengthen this provision, extending it to include commercial sales, created considerable controversy in 1976. Congress felt that the United States, as the world's leading arms supplier, prompted global instability at the cost of peace.

Congress had passed a separate two-year economic aid bill in 1975, but could not agree on a military aid bill by the end of the first session. When the foreign aid bill finally did pass it included both economic and military programs, but the $9 billion ceiling on total arms sales was dropped, as were the restrictions that would have prohibited the transfer of U.S. arms to a third country without U.S. approval, because Ford vetoed the bill.

Congress did create the Arms Control and Export Act (AECA) in 1976, which expanded its authority pertaining to U.S. arms sales, created the IMET program, and mandated the phase-out of MAP. Congress further prohibited arms transfers to any country (except in extraordinary circumstances) engaging in "a consistent pattern of gross violations of internationally recognized human rights," and required the president to make an annual evaluation for Congress on human rights conditions in countries where U.S. aid might go.[136] This was widely supported on Capitol Hill.

The Carter Administration

President James Carter indicated he would use economic support assistance as a foreign policy tool to strengthen the economic underpinnings of recipient nations to achieve global stability. Foreign military sales were to be used as an exceptional foreign policy instrument to help other governments meet their essential security needs by themselves—a Democratic reiteration of the Nixon Doctrine.[137] Carter believed that the overall purpose of security assistance was to assure peace and stability so nations could devote their full energies to development, while also advancing U.S. security interests.[138]

Carter also suggested that security assistance policies must address U.S. commitments to the defense needs and independence of friends and allies, fully reflect U.S. concern for basic human rights, and give substance to the administration's resolve to restrain the arms trade.[139] The goal of security assistance was to bring stability to troubled Third World regions.

Congress remained committed to human rights issues, which proved to overshadow and delay the foreign aid bill in 1977. At issue was a congressional proposal that required the administration to vote against loans from international lending organizations to Communist nations and those with poor human rights records.[140] It ended with a Carter compromise for a policy of flexibility with respect to human rights violations in certain countries. This brought congressional ire, particularly from House conservatives who favored a policy of uniformity.

During this debate several countries were earmarked for a cutoff of aid because of disregard for "internationally recognized human rights standards," including Brazil, El Salvador, Guatemala, Argentina, Ethiopia, and Uruguay. These alleged infractions, however, were viewed differently depending upon the country, and thus carried varying degrees of significance. For example, some countries would have entire FMS programs slashed for specific violations, while others might suffer only a "token" IMET cut for identical infractions. This cut to the heart of Carter's flexibility approach. In other words, Congress and the administration each developed ways of dealing with specific rights violators. A major influence on these decisions was that country's relationship to the United States and NATO (or its corresponding hemispheric value), with the bottom line usually being human rights. With such a policy, Carter hoped to exercise leverage over developing countries toward effecting increased pro-West leanings.

Most foreign aid this year was earmarked for the Middle East (65 percent) because of growing concerns over protecting Persian Gulf oil supplies as a vital U.S. interest. The Senate Committee on Foreign Relations reaffirmed its strong support of Israel, which was accorded "special treatment" status for arms sales. The Committee generally agreed, however, with the president in

> reaffirming that a policy of restraint in U.S. arms transfers, including arms sales ceilings, shall not impair Israel's deterrent strength or undermine the military balance in the Middle East.[141]

Another controversial issue was Carter's proposed sale of AWACS (airborne warning and control system) airplanes to Iran.[142] When the White House postponed congressional consideration of its proposal, the *Washington Star* commended the administration for wisely delaying "the moment of decision." Earlier, the *Washington Post* had urged the Congress to disapprove the sale. The administration then had sufficient time to line up support to insure that Congress would approve the sale, which it later did.[143]

The focus of the FY 1979 aid debate was repealing the three-year-old Turkish arms embargo.[144] While stopping short of an outright repeal, Congress criticized the general lack of progress toward a Cyprus settlement, a subject of intense interest during the authorization process, and instead passed a de facto repeal; full repeal would be granted upon "Presidential confirmation" that a full resumption of military cooperation with Turkey was in the national interest of the United States, and that Turkey was acting in "good faith" toward affecting a "just and peaceful settlement in Cyprus." Carter's approach to the Greek–Turkish dispute was middle-of-the-road, and the same way in which he approached his human rights policies—"carrot and stick" with the emphasis on the carrot. His perceived incoherence alienated many in Congress who believed that U.S. prestige and foreign policy suffered under his administration.

The *Washington Post* commended Carter and urged Congress to lift the embargo and give diplomacy "a chance to start healing the wounds in Cyprus." While "the embargo at its outset was a well-meant, legally mandated protest against the use of American arms for the occupation" of the island, "experience has proven it to be destructive of the purpose it was meant to serve—reducing the occupation." It now stands "simply as a hostile act against an ally, and one not in the slightest endorsed by any other NATO ally—except for Greece."[145]

In keeping with past practice, Congress included provisions in its FY 1979 legislation prohibiting security assistance to nations that violated human rights "unless the Secretary of State finds that extraordinary circumstances prevail which necessitate a continuation of aid." In other areas, the Senate renamed the "security supporting assistance" program the "Economic Support Fund" to more accurately reflect the actual use of the funds and "to provide budget support and development aid to countries of political importance to the United States." In the past, this particular program had drawn congressional criticism, who viewed it as simply a military aid reserve fund, disguised as economic aid. Many such criticisms, as in the past, accompanied domestic economic problems in the United States.

As in the recent past, most military and economic aid went to Israel. Egypt received nearly as much. Continued aid to this region was legitimized by administration requests and in congressional appropriations in terms of U.S. national security. Similarly, massive infusions of capital and weapons had been justified to Southeast Asia as recently as 1972.

Again, arms sales and high-technology weapon transfers continued to distress Congress. This year, the Committee on Appropriations (House) expressed hope that future sales to developing nations would be more closely monitored:

> In the past, the vast majority of sales have been targeted at the Middle East–Persian Gulf region. As a result, many . . . developing countries are spending huge amounts on their military establishment while their poor live with little prospect of improvement.[146]

The FY 1980 appropriation bill stalled in conference, so an emergency funding resolution was passed. Since this was effective for the entire year further action was not resumed. Although the subject of international lending organizations had troubled certain congressmen before, it had never actually delayed the passage of all foreign aid legislation to such an extent as it did in 1979. Other congressional concerns focused around aid to some recent arrivals to the human rights "violators club," namely, South Korea, the Philippines, Thailand, Panama, the Sudan, and Yemen. Aid to these countries was reduced, rather than terminated outright, as a means of symbolic censure. Congress again pressured the administration to phase out, as mandated in 1976, grant military assistance in favor of other reimbursable-type programs in order to relieve the burden placed on the Treasury for continued administration of such programs (there were similar trends in attitudes toward the IMET program).

Military aid to Turkey proved contentious this year, even though the U.S.–Turkey aid relationship went back decades. Historically, the Senate was more sensitive to Turkish considerations, while the House has tended to side with Greece. The Carter administration argued that grant military aid was necessary for Turkey to uphold its minimum NATO commitments. Congressional opposition argued that Turkey had shown insufficient "good faith" toward Greece with regard to settling the Cyprus issue. House and Senate conferees finally reached a compromise, which provided substantial aid to Greece as well, and gave a combination of loans and grants to Turkey (which made it the third largest recipient of U.S. assistance). In the end, however, it was all for naught. Despite this authorization, conferees were unable to compromise on an appropriation bill. So without the requisite program authority, the authorization did not amount to very much.

Pakistan, according to several reports in the 1970s, was apparently acquiring a nuclear weapons capability. These indications reached a peak in 1979, and the Carter administration responded by cutting off all aid. The *Washington Star* agreed that there was indeed no reason "for the United States to make it easier for Pakistan to join the [nuclear] club." In Los Angeles, however, the *Times* suggested that Washington should make it more apparent that it sympathizes with Pakistan's security concerns and "is prepared to help with economic and military aid if the nuclear issue can be worked out."[147]

An event that directly influenced the security assistance program was the Middle East peace treaty between Egypt and Israel. Part of the price of that peace were U.S. aid assurances to both nations, which would soon come to dominate program funding in the foreign aid legislation. Also, relations between Israel and the United States cooled when Secretary of State Cyrus Vance informed Congress that

Israel may have violated the 1952 military aid treaty when Israel attacked Lebanon with U.S. F-15 fighter aircraft. Also, Nicaragua's dictator, Anastasio Somoza resigned, and the coup in El Salvador this year, would have a critical impact on the role of security assistance as an instrument of U.S. policy.

After the Soviet invasion of Afghanistan in late 1979, President Carter, following the lead of Zbigniew Brzezinski, his assistant for National Security Affairs, began to address more directly his concern over Soviet hegemony. Carter indicated that the United States had to meet the Soviet threat and expressed his desire to halt Cuban-engendered communism in Central America, the Caribbean, and in Southeast Asia. Security assistance, therefore, remained an excellent investment for the United States. The essential problem, he suggested, was whether America was going to be able, short of military action, to compete successfully with the Soviet Union, "for the hearts and minds and friendship and trade of the developing nations of the earth."[148]

For the second year in a row Congress failed to pass a foreign aid appropriation bill, again requiring passage of an emergency funding resolution to continue the program. The most controversial proposal in 1980 concerned emergency economic aid to Nicaragua, after Somoza had been overthrown. House conservatives successfully delayed the request because the new Nicaraguan regime was mostly Communist.[149] Congress eventually authorized Carter's request and appropriated $75 million, but only after several restrictions were added.

Carter also argued for greater flexibility "to meet unforeseen foreign policy and security emergencies," such as the Soviet's invasion of Afghanistan, and Congress gave the president greater flexibility to provide military aid even if prohibited by law—provided he show that the aid is "vital to the national security interests of the United States." The authorization bill refined some of the restrictions on commercial arms sales and allowed for certain exemptions for U.S. allies and friends.

A Republican presidential and Senate victory in the 1980 elections created considerable confusion on Capitol Hill in the lame-duck session that followed. Little action on the military aid proposal occurred.

The Reagan Administration, 1981–1983

When Ronald Reagan entered the presidency one of his first actions was to issue a presidential directive that superseded the arms transfer policy of the Carter Administration (PD 13). Whereas Carter emphasized arms sales restrictions, the new Reagan administration would evaluate arms sales requests primarily in terms of their "net contribution to enhanced deterrence and defense." It would also consider whether the transfer will "promote mutual interests in countering externally supported aggression." No mention is made of human rights considerations. Moreover, the policy shift argues that past restrictions failed because there had been little or no interest in such limitations by the Soviet Union or the majority of other arms producing nations. Therefore, "the United States will not jeopardize its own security needs through a program of unilateral restraint."[150] Whereas the Carter administration viewed arms sales as "exceptional" instruments of foreign policy, the Reagan administration perceives their use as an essential element of the U.S. defense posture and an indispensible component of foreign policy.[151]

President Reagan emphasized in 1981 that security assistance was the principal means by which the United States contributed to the security and development needs of a wide range of less-favored countries. Such programs, he argued, were vital to U.S. foreign policy and national security interests, an essential complement to the U.S. defense effort and therefore directly enhanced U.S. security, and central to U.S. policy objectives. Their importance to U.S. security could not be exaggerated.[152]

The FY 1982 authorization bill was finally cleared for the new president after considerable bipartisan opposition over the administration's efforts to roll back various Vietnam-era restrictions to control executive branch foreign policy.[153] Congress continued to flex its legislative muscles and passed a bill with one provision that required the president to report secretly to Congress on any reasons he might have for waiving an aid ban for nations dealing in Uranium enrichment or reprocessing equipment. Congress gave itself veto power over any presidential waiver of an aid ban imposed under nonproliferation laws. Several papers, such as the *Washington Post* had decried administration proposals to relax aid restrictions to nations engaged in nuclear-weapons development. Perhaps the most important provision of this bill was one that allowed the president to waive the "Symington amendment"—this had banned aid to countries dealing in unsafeguarded nuclear-enrichment technology. This provision then cleared the way for a $3.2 billion economic and military aid package for Pakistan—one near and dear to Reagan.

Aid to El Salvador proved contentious in 1981 on Capitol Hill, primarily because the ghost of Vietnam hung over Congress as it considered the possibility of direct military involvement, human rights violations, Soviet–Cuban hegemony, and regional conflict in

Central America. President Reagan made the region a "vital U.S. interest," and Secretary of State Alexander Haig had drawn the line there, warning the Soviets not to interfere. As passed, the FY 1982 authorization bill urged "good faith" on the part of El Salvador to negotiate with a political settlement, reform human rights practices, and gain "control over" its armed forces, as conditions for U.S. aid.

The media expressed concern over rising U.S. aid commitments to Central America. The underlying fear was possible escalation to widespread conflict in the region. Moreover, there were clear references to Vietnam and parallels to Vietnam were drawn with El Salvador.

At the urging of Chairman Clement Zablocki, the Committee on Foreign Affairs recommended a two-year authorization bill with major funding increases, and reflected the administration's emphasis on military-related aid. Its Senate counterpart initially rejected a two-year authorization, arguing that it was unwise to set limits on aid so far in advance, but reconsidered it during conference where an authorization bill finally passed for FY 1982 and FY 1983.

A major congressional hurdle was Reagan's request for repealing the Clark amendment prohibiting covert aid to factions in Angola. The Senate Committee on Foreign Relations voted to repeal it, but included a congressional oversight provision. Its House counterpart, on the other hand, argued that "repeal would make the Angolans more reliant on the estimated 20,000 Cuban troops, which the U.S. wants out of Angola," and that U.S. intervention would harm prospects for peace in Namibia. Reagan's request was dropped during conference and was not pursued. Although the first regular foreign aid spending bill since 1978 was passed in 1981, major partisan and ideological differences erupted during congressional debates, primarily over the relative emphases placed on development aid and military assistance.

Against the backdrop of the largest defense buildup in U.S. peacetime history, a faltering domestic economy, historic budget deficits, and the dismantling of the social welfare program, the Reagan administration returned to Capitol Hill in 1982 and requested an even larger military assistance authorization than it had received the year before as part of a two-year authorization. Congress' reaction was not surprising—the request was not well-received and was therefore delayed. Congress remained in a budget austerity mood and sought large reductions and alterations in foreign aid.

Moreover, the administration found itself with major problems over aid to El Salvador, Guatemala, and other nations accused of human rights violations. In the media, El Salvador continued to dominate the attention of many across the country. Many papers argued that while the United States had interests at stake in Central America, the military-dominated solutions of the Reagan administration were not appropriate to the peaceful resolution of regional conflict. Furthermore, the *New York Times*, for example, decried the certification process as hypocritical, and demanded that Congress act firmly in opposing the administration.

Amid this controversy came the Israeli invasion of Lebanon and the massacre of civilians in Beirut. Before this the Senate Committee on Foreign Relations had recommended a contentious aid increase to Israel. For the most part, this increase went above and beyond Reagan's original request and caused the entire foreign aid process to stalemate. Many believed that approval of the increase would have amounted to tacit support of Israel's invasion. Meanwhile, the Reagan administration attempted, in a poorly coordinated manner, to bring pressure against this increase. This resulted in an Israeli verbal attack on the administration for attempting to cut the Senate-proposed increase.

Those such as the *Christian Science Monitor* argued that aid to Israel was not really the issue in the debate, but rather the expansion of Israeli territory, which only the United States could curtail. The paper urged Congress to demonstrate courage and statesmanship in opposing Prime Minister Begin's practices of annexing Arab lands.

In 1983 the United States was well on its way to a military buildup in Central America. Congress remained divided over U.S. policy in the region, and was deeply involved through military assistance to El Salvador, covert aid to Nicaraguan insurgents, and military training in Honduras. Liberals tried to ban such assistance outright and criticized the undue military emphasis of U.S. involvement, while the administration increased its commitments in Central America and lifted a five-year military air embargo against Guatemala for alleged improvement in its human rights record.

Aid to Israel also led the aid agenda. The Reagan administration was initially unsupportive of congressional increases of aid to Israel because, they argued, reprogramming efforts would result in funding levels to other countries being cut. Moreover, there continued major shifts from loans to grant-type aid to Israel (with strong congressional support), and with administration promises of more for FY 1985.

Other problems arose over reports of aid ineffectiveness in Africa (after decades of U.S. help), arms sales to Taiwan, Iraq, Jordan, and Saudi Arabia, concerns that the Pentagon was peddling arms to the world, accusations about lack of congressional consultation on key foreign policy issues, and criticism of nations who received U.S. aid, but failed to always support the United States. Human rights concerns were salient as well. Also, controversy erupted when it was suggested that the United States move some of its military bases from Greece to Turkey.

In this context, Secretary of State George Shultz appointed a bipartisan Commission on Security and Economic Assistance—the so-called Carlucci Commission—to restudy carefully the lack of aid support and what might be done to build a consensus policy. The Commission concluded that aid had become a polarized issue, budgetary problems have forced trade-offs between domestic and international programs, and the public no longer views aid as "coherently serving U.S. vital interests." It recommended to increase funding levels, build bipartisan support, increase concessionality, and bring all aid programs into a Mutual Development and Security Administration to report to the Secretary of State.[154] Although it was the first high-level review of aid in a decade, it did not receive wide attention.

In part this was due to the rise of a presidential commission on U.S. policy in Central America—the Kissinger Commission. It recommended a substantial five-year economic aid program to the region and emergency assistance to El Salvador to thwart the spread of communism in the region. While it was touted as bipartisan, it failed to attract bipartisan support. The *New York Times* called it "pure Reagan doctrine." It will scarcely end the debate. So too the *Washington Post* predicted the debate over Central American policy will only likely be intensified by the Kissinger report. In truth, the United States stands at a critical juncture. What is done in Central America by the Reagan administration will be noted by future analysts as a critical juncture in U.S. history.

Conclusion

Here we stand today. It is unlikely that bipartisanship will prevail, or that Congress will relinquish its concern over the direction of U.S. policy overseas, or that the media will begin to reflect any differently in the near future. In the meantime, the executive branch must deal with allies, friends, and opponents abroad in a coherent manner. The following analysis of the history of perceptions of security assistance is intended to come to a clearer understanding of the program's basic problems.

For the past twenty-seven years there has been remarkable continuity in executive branch rationale for the security assistance program. These perceptions have not changed significantly since the mid-1950s. First and foremost among the dominant themes is that anticommunism, whether explicit or implicit, has been a driving force for security assistance. This theme was strong and explicit under presidents Eisenhower, Kennedy, and Johnson. It then waned (but did not disappear) during détente under Nixon, Ford, and Carter (through 1979), waxed strong again toward the end of Carter's term (1980), and has become preeminent under Reagan. Every administration since the late-1950s has, therefore, viewed security assistance as vital to the conduct of U.S. foreign and defense policy, arguing that it plays an integral role in global security.

Security assistance is seen by the executive branch as a shield behind which political, economic, and social development could occur throughout the world. The rationale is that a community of independent and prosperous nations is the best long-term guarantee of a secure United States in a peaceful world. Security assistance strengthens the defense capabilities and economies of friends and allies. In addition, this military aid is perceived to be more efficient and less costly than regular defense expenditures for U.S. security.

There has been an evolution of program thought, however, made explicit in the Nixon Doctrine—the prime objective of security assistance is to help those countries assume the responsibility of their own defense and thus help reduce the need for a U.S. presence abroad. Presidents Eisenhower, Kennedy, and Johnson, however, paved the way for the Nixon Doctrine, which theme continued under the Ford and Carter administrations. This emphasis is not as evident in the Reagan administration, however, which has a tendency to "go it alone" and not to embrace this concept as much as its predecessors.

Every president also makes it clear to Congress that his security assistance request constitutes "the minimum essential contribution to world peace," and that any reductions or variations from his proposal will "not bode well for global security." Upon entering office, every administration sees fit to call for "new directions," a "fresh approach," or a "new beginning." In reality, they are asking for essentially the same things. These include requests for multi-year authorizations, the separation of security assistance from economic aid, and demands for greater program efficiency, better management, and policy coordination. The two authorizing committees in Congress, however, cannot be expected to diminish their jurisdiction by turning over to the Departments of State or Defense any significant part of their program authority. These committees will continue to insist on being involved regularly in foreign policy. The security assistance process perhaps provides Congress' only real opportunity to do so.

There was a shift in emphasis away from grant aid in the mid-1960s (that had begun earlier in the 1950s), to its eventual mandated end that was legislated in the mid-1970s. During this period there was a commensurate increase in foreign military sales and credits. Most recently, however, there appears to be a growing consensus favoring a return to grants on a larger scale. In part, this has grown out of the recognition that many nations are becoming unable to meet their debts. In the future, it is likely that we will see a decrease in emphasis on loans and an increase in forms of grant aid as Congress attempts to deal realistically with the current unstable state of the international monetary system.

In dealing with Congress, every president appeals to "bipartisan support" the program has received historically. In addition, presidents have been willing to cite "success" stories such as Western Europe, Greece, Turkey, South Korea, and even South Vietnam and Iran, before the last two countries were taken over by hostile governments.

There has been an evolution of thought on arms sales and transfers. Initial concern arose in the Johnson administration over providing sophisticated weapons to Third World countries. Johnson himself imposed restrictions as did the Congress. Nixon continued to express some concern over these same issues, but argued for greater flexibility. Nevertheless, Congress continued to add provisions to foreign aid bills that restricted arms sales. President Ford experienced the greatest difficulty in this area, eventually challenging the constitutionality of several legislative restrictions, specifically during the Turkish arms embargo. Under Carter, the policy shifted to restrict the flow of arms severely and to attempt to influence human rights practices in other nations. Carter not only upset Congress because of his perceived inconsistencies, but he also met with little success in curtailing the global arms sales business. Reagan has entered office determined to change the arms transfer policies of the Carter years. He has largely succeeded.

Attitudes on human rights have also evolved and changed in the executive branch. In large part, however, these have followed the lead of Congress. Ford acknowledged the historical role of the United States in the protection of basic human rights, but argued that congressional restrictions on military aid (because of human rights abuses, for example) were ineffective. Carter, on the other hand, used observance of human rights as a major criterion for provision of security assistance, but ran into congressional trouble when this criterion was not applied equally in all instances. The Reagan administration perceives the publicized denial of security assistance on the grounds of human rights violations as wholly ineffective and counterproductive.

Finally, every administration expresses displeasure with congressional handling of the military aid program, especially over aid levels and restrictive amendments. This theme reached its zenith in the late-Nixon period and under Ford, both of whom raised questions of constitutionality in their dealings with Congress. Carter attempted to work with Congress to improve these relations, but failed, and the restrictions continued. Reagan has successfully sought repeal of certain limitations, but the Congress continues to exercise significant influence on U.S. policy through the security assistance program.

In Congress, as in the executive branch, many of the same arguments are used year after year. But, the weight of those arguments has shifted. In the early years, Congress was generally supportive. Over time, particularly through the decade of the Vietnam War, Congress moved toward selectivity, rather than general support, and skepticism about many aspects of the program grew. But, it is important to recognize that there has always been a consensus (although not always strongly explicit) that the program is important to U.S. interests and necessary to the conduct of U.S.foreign policy.

As for other themes, Congress is always concerned over waste, fraud, abuse, and program mismanagement. In addition, Congress shows great reluctance to emphasize military aid over development assistance. A theme stemming from the times (late-1950s and early-1960s)—that foreign assistance adversely affects the U.S. balance of payments—coincided with a national preoccupation over this issue. Today, while the theme is similar, the concern is slightly different—it has to do with the national debt. Congress is also always concerned that U.S. allies do not share in the burden of global defense proportionately.

Another theme that has grown stronger over time, particularly since Vietnam, is that the United States is overcommitted in the world and that security assistance inevitably leads to increased commitments and possible U.S. military involvement. The Congress generally agrees that foreign aid, particularly military aid, has been and remains an essential tool for exercising influence over other nations, however, even though this may not hold true. More recently, the general feeling is that U.S. leverage outweighs the negative effects of arms sales.

The media, it appears, have changed more over time than either the Congress or the executive branch. In the early years, newspapers such as the *New York Times, Christian Science Monitor, Washington Post,* and the *Washington Star* (the more influential of the Capital's two major papers at the time), were strongly supportive of military assistance. Any negative congressional views were decried. Media opposition in those years came from papers like the *Chicago Tribune* (known for its isolationist impulses) and the *Wall Street Journal* (known for its business conservatism).

The Vietnam War produced a far more pronounced and lasting change in media views. Media reporting became more knowledgeable and discriminative. In the late 1960s and early 1970s, the emphasis in the media was placed on calls for program reform. The distinctions between security and economic assistance received more attention in the 1970s than it had ever had.

By the mid-1970s, newspapers such as the *Christian Science Monitor* expressed opposition to specific program aspects. Arms sales, for example, commanded particular attention because they were perceived as contributing to the global arms race; the consequence of which was renewed regional conflicts. In some instances it was believed that too much emphasis was placed on military solutions to social, political, and economic problems, as opposed to economic and political solutions.

More recently, the media have paid closer attention to security assistance matters than ever before. It is not uncommon to find detailed articles written on the political-economic and military implications of U.S. aid efforts throughout the world. Since the media have become more sophisticated in their analyses it is no longer safe to assume that any one particular newspaper will take a position in support of or in opposition to congressional or executive branch actions. The media have developed their own views as to how foreign policy should be run and do not blindly support one branch of government over the other. They implicitly acknowledge, however, that security assistance plays a legitimate role in the conduct of U.S. foreign policy. However, such aid should not be used indiscriminately.

Finally, the question of partisanship in the program needs to be considered. One good way to analyze this is to compare the floor and conference votes on the foreign assistance authorizations and appropriation bills with the index of overall support for the president compiled by the *Congressional Quarterly Almanac.*

As one might expect, overall presidential support from 1959 to 1964 was largely from his own political party. Both parties in the Senate, however, demonstrated greater support for foreign assistance, particularly the Republicans, than for the overall program of the administration. In the House, the Democrats showed consistently high and steady support for the authorization bill as well. House Republican support of foreign assistance, however, declined steadily below general presidential support.

Through 1965, both parties in the Senate had relatively high support for foreign assistance appropriations, despite low, yet gradually rising, overall Republican support of the president. Similarly, House Democrats showed consistently high support for the program through 1966, while Republican support gradually declined.

From 1965 to 1975, partisanship concerning military aid is again clear. Democratic support declined (sharply in the House) through the mid-1970s, when it stabilized at fairly low levels. Conversely, Republican support of President Nixon rose through 1970 and declined after 1972–1973. Meanwhile, Democratic support for military aid paralleled the general party decline in presidential support, but still remained above it. Senate Republican support for the program similarly paralleled using general support, yet remained below Democratic support of the foreign assistance program. Republican support on the appropriation bills, however, was higher than the Democrats. While House Republican support of aid gradually increased, it remained well below this group's overall support of the president. Democratic support for aid (authorizations and appropriations) gradually declined, yet remained well above similar Republican support.

In this most recent period (1975–1983), there is also the expected degree of partisan support of the president. Again, however, support for the foreign assistance program is not so clearly partisan. Since 1959 the Democrats have shown stronger support for foreign assistance specifically, than for the overall program of the president, regardless of party. The only exception occurred in the late-1970s when several, solely military aid bills were supported more by the Republicans than by the Democrats, even though the latter gave higher support than usual during this period. Senate Democrats supported the appropriation bill again more than they supported the president overall, while Republican support was not high and fell below overall presidential support. In the House, there were mixed results throughout this period.

Upon closer examination, however, partisanship questions do not fully address support for or opposition to military assistance.

Ideology plays perhaps a stronger role. In the early period, many conservatives opposed such aid because of domestic economic rationales, while liberals extolled the program as part of the new world role of the United States. The Vietnam War disillusioned many liberals who believed that such assistance was still important to U.S. foreign and defense policy, but recognized its limitations. Military assistance cannot resolve fundamental political and economic inequities in many Third World settings. On the other hand, conservatives of both parties believe that enhanced military assistance can contain communism and allow political cultures and economies to grow and mature.

There are three broad groups today. In the House, there are some who will support aid under certain circumstances. One part (mostly Democrats) supports economic aid, while the other (mostly Republicans) supports military assistance. A second group (mostly conservatives) opposes aid on the grounds that it is a wasted program and cannot be helpful. Some liberals also belong to this group. A third group is somewhat ambivalent and can be influenced more readily by public opinion, from interest groups, or ethnic constituencies.

In conclusion, when one reviews the attitudes of Congress over time as reflected in public statements and when one examines the proliferation of restrictive amendments to foreign aid bills, one detects a feeling that Congress perceives that it has not been able to participate sufficiently early in the process to help formulate the program. Therefore, Congress feels the necessity of applying restrictions where, if it had been involved earlier, might not have done so. If we examine the record we find that Congress generally seeks amendments that are mostly remedial in nature. If the executive branch will recognize this and seek to address these perennial congressional concerns it is likely that a better security assistance program will result. Moreover, it is likely that a better foreign policy will result because of this greater consensus.

Notes

1. "Military assistance," in this paper, is defined as (1) grant programs including MAP, MAP Excess, MASF (Military Assistance Service Fund—this refers to all defense articles and defense services transferred to foreign countries under the authority contained in the Department of Defense Appropriations Act from FY 1966 to 1975; it was used for the war in Southeast Asia), MASF Excess, MASF Training, IMET, and FMS credits waived, and (2) FMS credit programs including Direct and Guaranty financing (excludes

FMS credits waived, FY 1974 to FY 1982 only). "Security assistance" is defined herein as military assistance plus economic support. Officially, it is that "group of programs authorized by the Foreign Assistance Act of 1961, as amended, and the Arms Export Control Act of 1976, as amended, or other related statutes by which the United States provides defense articles, military training, and other defense related services, by grant, credit, or cash sales, in furtherance of national policies and objectives." U.S. Department of Defense, The Joint Chiefs of Staff, *Dictionary of Military and Associated Terms* (cited hereafter as JCS Pub. 1) (Washington, D.C.: U.S. GPO, 1 June 1979), p. 306.

2. The *Public Papers of the President, Congressional Record,* committee hearings, and major newspaper editorials for the period 1959 through 1983 were used as the basis of this chapter. The years 1959–1960 were chosen to represent not only the general sentiments of the 1950s regarding military assistance, but also because they began to show that a period of transition was beginning to occur.

3. "That portion of the U.S. security assistance authorized by the Foreign Assistance Act of 1961, as amended, which provides defense articles to recipients on a nonreimbursable (grant) basis." JCS Pub. 1, p. 214. MAP is the dollar amount of these defense articles, "other than training, [which] have been provided to eligible foreign governments on a grant basis." *Congressional Presentation Document* (hereafter CPD), Security Assistance Programs, FY 1983 (Washington, D.C.: U.S. GPO, 1982), p. 2.

4. "Formal or informal instruction provided to foreign military students, units, and forces on a nonreimbursable (grant) basis by officers or employees of the United States, contract technicians, and contractors. Instruction may include correspondence courses, technical, educational, or informational publications and media of all kinds." JCS Pub. 1, p. 182. More recently, it has been defined as training "provided in the United States, in U.S. schools in Panama, and, in some instances, either in U.S. military facilities overseas or by the use of mobile training teams, to selected foreign military and related civilian personnel on a grant basis." CPD, p. 2.

5. "That portion of the U.S. security assistance authorized by the Foreign Assistance Act of 1961, as amended, and the Arms Export Control Act of 1976, as amended. This assistance differs from MAP and IMET in that the recipient provides reimbursement for defense articles and services transferred." JCS Pub. 1, p. 144. It is the "financing program by which [the United States furnishes] credits and loan repayment guaranties to enable eligible foreign governments to purchase defense articles and training." CPD, p. 2.

6. It has also been called "defense support" and "security supporting assistance"—the program by which "economic assistance is provided on a loan or grant basis, to selected foreign governments having unique security problems. The funds are used to finance imports of commodities, capital, or technical assistance in accordance with terms of a bilateral agreement; counterpart funds thereby generated may be used as budgetary support. These funds enable a recipient to devote more of its resources to defense

and security purposes than it otherwise could do without serious economic or political consequences." JCS Pub. 1, p. 307. It is "economic assistance . . . provided on a grant and loan basis to selected countries of special political and security interest to the U.S." CPD, p. 2.

7. The program "by which grant assistance is designated for programs designed specifically for peacekeeping operations. In past years, this included the Sinai Support Mission (SSM) and the U.S. contribution to the UN Force in Cyprus (UNFICYP)." Ibid.

8. *The Management of Security Assistance,* 2d ed. (Wright Patterson AFB, Ohio: Defense Institute of Security Assistance Management, May 1981), pp. 3-1 and 3-2.

9. Ibid., p. 3-5.

10. Ibid., pp. 5-2 and 5-3.

11. In the House, these subcommittees include: International Security and Scientific Affairs; International Operations; Europe and the Middle East; Asian and Pacific Affairs; International Economic Policy and Trade; Western Hemisphere Affairs; Africa; and International Organizations. In the Senate: International Economic Policy; Arms Control, Oceans, International Operations, and Environment; African Affairs; Near Eastern and South Eastern Affairs; and Western Hemisphere Affairs.

12. Aaron Wildavsky, *The Politics of the Budgetary Process,* 3d ed. (Boston: Little, Brown, and Company, 1979), p. 61.

13. Amos A. Jordan and William J. Taylor, Jr., *American National Security* (Baltimore: Johns Hopkins University Press, 1981), p. 255.

14. See for example, U.S. Comptroller General, *Examination of the Military Assistance Program,* House Committee on Foreign Affairs, 85th Cong., 1st Sess., March 1957; U.S. Comptroller General, *Review of the Pricing of Materiel to the Military Assistance Program by the Military Departments,* General Accounting Office, Report No. B-133288, 1960; U.S. Congress, House Committee on Government Operations, Subcommittee on International Operations, *Use of Defense Support Funds for Economic and Political Purposes,* 85th Cong., 2d Sess., 1958; U.S. Congress, House Committee on Government Operations, *Use of Defense Support Funds for Economic and Political Purposes,* 85th Cong., 2d Sess., Report No. 1374, 1958; U.S. Congress, House Committee on Foreign Affairs, *Report of Special Study Mission to Asia, Western Pacific, Middle East, Southern Europe, and North Africa,* 86th Cong., 1st Sess., Report No. 1386, 1959; U.S. Congress, House Committee on Foreign Affairs, *Criticisms of the Foreign Aid Program and Comments by State, ICA, and Defense,* 86th Cong., 1st Sess., 1959; U.S. Congress, Special Committee to Study the Foreign Aid Program, *Hearings, the Foreign Aid Program,* 85th Cong., 1st Sess., 1957; U.S. Congress, Special Committee to Study the Foreign Aid Program, *Foreign Aid Program, Compilation of Studies and Surveys,* 85th Cong., 1st Sess., Document No. 52, 1957; U.S. Congress, Special Committee to Study the Foreign Aid Program, *Report on Foreign Aid,* 85th Cong., 1st Sess., Report No. 300, 1957; U.S. Congress, Senate Committee on Foreign Relations, *Compilation of Studies on United*

States Foreign Policy, 2 vols., 86th Cong., 2d Sess., 1960; U.S. Department of State, *Report to the Congress on Grant Economic Assistance Relating to Defense Support and Special Assistance Programs, Mutual Security Program,* March, 1960; U.S International Cooperation Administration, Office of Statistics and Reports, *U.S. External Assistance, July 1, 1954 Through June 30, 1959,* March, 1960; U.S. President Eisenhower, The President's Citizen Advisers on the National Security Program (Fairless Committee), *Report,* March 1957.

15. The interim reports, conclusions, and recommendations of the Draper Committee are found in U.S. President Eisenhower, The President's Committee to Study the Military Assistance Program, *Composite Report* (Vol. 1) and *Supplement to the Composite Report* (Vol. 2), August 1959.

16. "Special Message to the Congress on the Mutual Security Program, March 13, 1959," *Public Papers of the President of the United States: Eisenhower, 1950* [cited hereafter as *Public Papers of the President*] (Washington, D.C.: U.S. GPO, 1960, p. 55).

17. *New York Times,* March 19, 1959, p. 32.

18. *Christian Science Monitor,* March 12 and 16, 1959; *Washington Star,* March 15, 1959.

19. *Chicago Tribune,* March 14, 1959.

20. *Wall Street Journal,* April 29, 1959, p. E-1, and August 24, 1959.

21. *Los Angeles Times,* July 24, 1959.

22. U.S. Congress, House, *Mutual Security Act of 1959, Report of the Committee on Foreign Affairs on H.R. 7500,* 86th Cong., 1st Sess., June 5, 1959.

23. U.S. Congress, Senate, *The Mutual Security Act of 1959, Report of the Committee on Foreign Relations on S. 1451, with Minority Views,* 86th Cong., 1st Sess., June 22, 1959.

24. *New York Times,* June 25, 1959, p. 28, and July 18, 1959, p. 2.

25. Ibid., July 24, 1959, p. 24.

26. See the *Washington Post,* March 14, 1959, p. 22, and July 26, 1959, pp. IV-8, E-1.

27. *Chicago Tribune,* August 21, 1959, p. 5.

28. *Chicago Sun-Times,* February 17, 1960, p. 27.

29. *Christian Science Monitor,* March 4, 1960.

30. U.S. Congress, Senate, *Mutual Security Act of 1960, Hearings on S. 3058,* 86th Cong., 2d Sess., March 22–April 5, 1960.

31. *Wall Street Journal,* May 4, 1960, p. 12; *Chicago Tribune,* May 4, 1960, p. 16.

32. "Address at a Dinner Sponsored by the Committee for International Economic Growth to Strengthen the Frontiers of Freedom, May 2, 1960," *Public Papers of the President: Eisenhower,* pp. 378–384.

33. These series are referred to in U.S. Congress, House, *Hearings, Mutual Security Appropriations for 1961 (and Related Agencies), before the Subcommittee of the Committee on Appropriations,* 86th Cong., 2d Sess., 1960, pp. 2288–2292.

34. U.S. Cognress, House, *Mutual Security and Related Agencies Appropriations bill, 1961, Report from the Committee on Appropriations to accompany H.R. 12619,* 86th Cong., 2d Sess., June 13, 1960.

35. *Chicago Sun-Times,* June 14, 1960, p. 27.

36. *New York Times,* June 15, 1960, p. 40; *Los Angeles Times,* June 15, 1960.

37. *New York Times,* August 26, 1960, p. A-24.

38. "Special Message to the Congress on Foreign Aid, March 22, 1961," *Public Papers of the President: Kennedy,* pp. 203–212.

39. Donald Bruce Johnson, comp., *National Party Platforms, Vol. II, 1960–1976* (Chicago: University of Illinois Press, 1977), p. 601.

40. "Special Message," *Public Papers of the President: Kennedy,* pp. 203–212.

41. *New York Times,* March 24, 1961, p. 30; *Baltimore Sun,* March 23, 1961, p. 18.

42. *St. Louis Post-Dispatch,* March 22, 1961, p. 2-C.

43. *New York Times,* July 9, 1961, p. 6E.

44. *Salt Lake Tribune,* March 24, 1961, p. 14.

45. *Washington Star,* May 26, 1961, p. 14; *Salt Lake Tribune,* May 26, 1961, p. 14-A.

46. U.S. Congress, House, *Hearings, Foreign Assistance and Related Agencies Appropriation Bill, 1962,* 87th Cong., 1st Sess., September 1, 1961.

47. *New York Times,* September 2, 1961, p. 14.

48. 75 Stat. 424–465 (Foreign Assistance Act of 1961, PL 87-195).

49. "Special Message to the Congress on Foreign Aid, March 13, 1962," *Public Papers of the President: Kennedy,* pp. 214–217.

50. *Washington Post,* March 15, 1962, p. A-22; *Wall Street Journal,* March 16, 1962, p. 6; *Chicago Tribune,* March 14, 1962, p. 16; *New York Times,* March 14, 1962, p. 38.

51. "Presidential News Conference, July 23, 1962," *Public Papers of the President: Kennedy,* p. 570. See also "Annual Message to the Congress on the State of the Union, January 11, 1962," *Public Papers of the President: Kennedy,* p. 14.

52. U.S. Congress, Senate, *Foreign Assistance Act of 1962, Hearings on S. 2996, before the Committee on Foreign Relations,* 87th Cong., 2d Sess., April 5–18, 1962.

53. 76 Stat 255-63 (Foreign Assistance Act of 1962, PL 87-565). This was the first time that aid to communist countries was prohibited by name.

54. U.S. Congress, House Committee on Foreign Affairs, *Report of Staff Survey Team of the Subcommittee for Review of Mutual Security Programs on U.S. Aid to Korea, Vietnam, and Turkey,* 87th Cong., 2d Sess., February 22, 1962.

55. "President's News Conference of March 14, 1962," *Public Papers of the President: Kennedy,* p. 89. (Italics added.)

56. U.S. Department of State, *Report to the President of the United States from the Committee to Strengthen the Security of the Free World,*

Scope and Distribution of U.S. Military and Economic Assistance Program, March 20, 1963 (Washington, D.C.: U.S. Department of State, 1963).

57. *Washington Star,* March 25, 1963, p. A-10.

58. *Wall Street Journal,* March 26, 1963, p. 18.

59. *Washington Post,* March 24, 1963, p. 6; *New York Times,* March 27, 1963, p. E-6; *Christian Science Monitor,* March 23, 1963, p. E-1; *Chicago Sun-Times,* March 26, 1963, p. 23.

60. "Message on Free World Defense and Assistance Programs, April 2, 1963," *Public Papers of the President: Kennedy.*

61. Theodore C. Sorensen, *Kennedy* (New York: Harper & Row, 1965), p. 393.

62. *Los Angeles Times,* March 20, 1964, p. 20; *Atlanta Constitution,* March 21, 1964, p. 4; *Wall Street Journal,* March 20, 1964.

63. U.S. Congress, Senate Committee on Foreign Relations, *Foreign Assistance Act of 1963, Hearings on S. 1276,* 88th Cong., 1st Sess., June 11–July 11, 1963.

64. U.S. Congress, Senate Committee on Appropriations, *Hearings, Foreign Assistance and Related Appropriations for 1963,* 88th Cong., 1st Sess.

65. U.S. Congress, House, *Additional Appropriations for Military Requirements in Vietnam, Message from President of the United States, Transmitting Request for Additional Appropriations to Meet Mounting Military Requirements in Vietnam,* 89th Cong., 1st Sess., Document No. 157, May 4, 1965.

66. *New York Times,* January 7, 1965, p. 30.

67. Ibid., January 28, 1965, p. 28, and February 24, 1965, p. 10.

68. "Special Message to Congress on Foreign Aid, January 14, 1965," *Public Papers of the President: Johnson,* pp. 44–50.

69. See note 65.

70. *New York Times,* May 5, 1965, p. 1 and May 9, 1965, p. 12-B.

71. *Wall Street Journal,* May 5, 1965, p. 3.

72. See note 65.

73. "Special Message to the Congress on the Foreign Aid Program, February 1, 1966," *Public Papers of the President: Johnson,* pp. 117, 121.

74. *New York Times,* February 2, 1966, p. 33.

75. *Christian Science Monitor,* February 4, 1966, p. 18; *Wall Street Journal,* February 4, 1966, p. 10; *Chicago Tribune,* February 2, 1966, p. 20.

76. U.S. Congress, Senate Committee on Foreign Relations, *Hearings, Foreign Assistance Act of 1966, on S. 2859 and S. 2861,* 89th Cong., 2d Sess., April 6–May 11, 1966; *Hearings, Supplemental Foreign Assistance for FY 1966, Vietnam, on S. 2793 (pt. 1),* 89th Cong., 2d Sess., January 28–February 18, 1966.

77. U.S. Congress, Senate, *Foreign Assistance Act of 1966. Report of the Committee on Foreign Relations, together with Individual Views,* 89th Cong., 2d Sess.

78. U.S. Congress, House Committee on Foreign Affairs, *Foreign Assistance Act of 1966, Hearings on H.R. 12449 and H.R. 12450,* 89th Cong.,

2d Sess., March 16–May 17, 1966; *Foreign Assistance Act of 1966. Report of Committee on Foreign Affairs on H.R. 15750,* Report No. 1651, June 23, 1966.

79. U.S. Congress, Senate, *Military Assistance and Sales Act. Report of Committee on Foreign Relations on S. 3583, with Minority Views,* 89th Cong., Report No. 1358, July 7, 1966.

80. U.S. Congress, Senate, *Congressional Record,* 89th Cong., 2d Sess., October 7, 1966, 112, pt. 19.

81. "Special Message to Congress on Foreign Aid, February 9, 1967," *Public Papers of the President: Johnson,* p. 164.

82. *New York Times,* January 17, 1967, p. 38.

83. Ibid., February 18, 1967, p. 28.

84. See U.S. Congress, Senate Committee on Foreign Relations, *Foreign Assistance Act of 1967, Hearings on S. 1872,* 90th Cong., 1st Sess., June 12–July 26, 1967; *Foreign Assistance Act of 1967. Report, together with Individual Views of Committee on Foreign Relations on S. 1872,* Report No. 499, August 9, 1967; Senate Committee on Appropriations, *Foreign Assistance and Related Agencies Appropriations for FY 1968, Hearings,* 90th Cong., 1st Sess.; House Committee on Foreign Affairs, *Foreign Assistance Act of 1967, Hearings on H.R. 7099,* 90th Cong., 1st Sess., April 4–June 8, 1967; *Foreign Assistance Act of 1967. Report of the Committee on Foreign Affairs together with Minority Views and Additional Views on H.R. 12048,* Report No. 551, August 11, 1967; House Committee on Appropriations, *Foreign Assistance and Related Agencies Appropriations for 1968, Hearings before the Subcommittee on Foreign Operations,* 90th Cong., 1st Sess.

85. U.S. Congress, Senate, *Arms Sales and Foreign Policy, Staff Study, Committee on Foreign Relations,* 90th Cong., 1st Sess., Committee Print, January 25, 1967.

86. See *New York Times,* July 19, 1967, p. 1 and August 27, 1967, p. IV-2.

87. *Washington Post,* February 10, 1968, p. A-12.

88. *Wall Street Journal,* February 9, 1968, p. 10.

89. U.S. Congress, House Committee on Foreign Affairs, *Foreign Assistance Act of 1968, Hearings on H.R. 15363,* 90th Cong., 2d Sess., February 28–May 2, 1968.

90. *Washington Star,* February 10, 1968, p. A-4.

91. See U.S. Congress, Senate Committee on Foreign Relations, *Foreign Assistance Act of 1969, Hearings,* 90th Cong., 2d Sess., February–June 1968.

92. *New York Times,* March 12, 1968, p. 42.

93. U.S. Congress, Senate Committee on Foreign Relations, *Foreign Military Sales, Hearings on S. 3092,* 90th Cong., 2d Sess., June 20, 1968; House Committee on Foreign Affairs, *Foreign Military Sales Act, Hearings on H.R. 15681,* 90th Cong., 2d Sess., June 26–27, 1968.

94. 82 Stat. 1320 (Foreign Military Sales Act of 1968, PL 90-629).

95. International Development Agency, *Developing Assistance in New*

Administration, Report of President's General Advisory Committee on Foreign Assistance Program, October 25, 1968 (Washington, D.C.: U.S. Department of State, 1969).

96. "Special Message to Congress Proposing Reform of Foreign Assistance Program, September 15, 1970," *Public Papers of the President: Nixon,* p. 746.

97. U.S. Congress, Senate Committee on Foreign Relations, *Foreign Assistance Act of 1969, Hearings on S. 2347,* 91st Cong., 1st Sess., July 14–August 6, 1969; House Committee on Foreign Affairs, *Foreign Assistance Act of 1969, Hearings on H.R. 11792,* 91st Cong., 1st Sess., June 9–August 1, 1969; House Committee on Appropriations, *Foreign Assistance and Related Agencies Appropriations for 1970, Hearings before the Subcommittee,* 91st Cong., 1st Sess.

98. *U.S. Foreign Assistance in the 1970s, New Approach, Report to the President from the Task Force on International Development,* March 4, 1970 (Washington, D.C.: The White House, 1970).

99. *Wall Street Journal,* March 12, 1970.

100. *New York Times,* March 12, 1970.

101. *Chicago Tribune,* March 10, 1970.

102. *San Francisco Chronicle,* May 13, 1970; *Pittsburgh Post-Gazette,* May 14, 1970.

103. *Washington Post,* June 8, 1970.

104. "Special Message to Congress Proposing Reform of Foreign Assistance Program, April 21, 1971," *Public Papers of the President: Nixon,* pp. 564–67.

105. U.S. Congress, Senate Committee on Foreign Relations, *Foreign Assistance Legislation, FY 1972, Hearings on S. 1656 and S. 1657,* 92d Cong., 1st Sess.: *Providing for Military and Related Assistance Authorization for 1972. Report together with Supplemental Views from Committee on Foreign Relations to Accompany S. 2819,* Report No. 431, November 8, 1971; House Committee on Appropriations, *Foreign Assistance and Related Agencies Appropriations, Hearings before Subcommittee,* 92d Cong., 1st Sess.

106. *New York Times,* January 10, 1971.

107. *Denver Post,* January 6, 1971.

108. "Statement by Press Secretary Ronald L. Ziegler, released by White House, October 7, 1971," printed in *Weekly Compilations of Presidential Documents,* vol. 7, p. 1457.

109. *Boston Globe,* November 2, 1971.

110. *New York Times,* November 1, 1971.

111. *Wall Street Journal,* November 2, 1971.

112. *Baltimore Sun,* July 26, 1972.

113. *Washington Post,* July 24, 1972.

114. *New York Times,* July 28, 1972.

115. See U.S. Congress, Senate, *Emergency Military Assistance for Israel and Cambodia, Hearings before the Senate Committee on Foreign Relations on S. 2692 and H.R. 11088,* 93d Cong., 1st Sess., December 13,

1973; *Providing Emergency Security Assistance Authority for Israel and Cambodia. Report together with Individual Views from Committee on Foreign Relations to accompany H.R. 11088,* Report No. 657, 93d Cong., December 19, 1973; PL 93-199.

116. *Christian Science Monitor,* June 9, 1973.

117. *Boston Globe,* June 9, 1973.

118. *Washington Post,* June 10, 1973.

119. *Los Angeles Times,* June 5, 1973.

120. "Special Message to Congress Transmitting Proposed Legislation for Funding of Foreign Assistance Programs in FY 1975," *Public Papers of the President: Nixon,* p. 374.

121. Kegley and Wittkopf, *Patterns,* p. 398.

122. *Washington Post,* October 10, 1974; *Wall Street Journal,* September 26, 1974.

123. U.S. Congress, Senate, *Foreign Assistance Act of 1974. Report together with Additional Views from Committee on Foreign Relations to Accompany S. 3394,* 93d Cong., 2d Sess., September 3, 1974.

124. Ibid.

125. See Richard F. Grimmett, *Trends in Conventional Arms Transfers to the Third World by Major Supplier,* Congressional Research Service Report No. 84-82F, May 7, 1984.

126. *Birmingham News,* February 18, 1975; *Philadelphia Inquirer,* February 18, 1975.

127. *Salt Lake Tribune,* February 16, 1975.

128. "Statement on Suspension of U.S. Military Assistance to Turkey, February 5, 1975," *Public Papers of the President: Ford,* p. 196.

129. "Letter to Speaker of the House Urging Military and Economic Assistance for Cambodia, May 25, 1975," *Public Papers of the President: Ford,* p. 280.

130. *Washington Post,* February 8, 1975.

131. *Seattle Times,* February 6, 1975.

132. "Remarks on Senate Action to Prohibit United States Assistance to Angola, December 19, 1975," *Public Papers of the President: Ford,* p. 1981.

133. *Washington Post,* January 15, 1976.

134. *Providence Journal,* February 4, 1976.

135. Andrew J. Pierre, *The Global Politics of Arms Sales* (Princeton: Princeton University Press, 1982).

136. 90 Stat 729 (International Security Assistance and Arms Export Control Act of 1976, PL 94-329).

137. "Conventional Arms Transfer Policy, May 19, 1977 [known as PD-13]," *Public Papers of the President: Carter,* pp. 931–932.

138. "Foreign Assistance Programs: Message to Congress, March 17, 1977," Ibid., p. 457.

139. "Security Assistance Programs, Letter to the Speaker of the House, March 28, 1977," Ibid., p. 524.

140. See U.S. Congress, House, *Foreign Assistance Legislation for FY*

1978, Hearings before the Committee on International Relations, 95th Cong., 1st Sess., February 22–April 28, 1977; Senate, *Foreign Assistance and Related Programs Appropriation for FY 1978, before the Subcommittee of the Committee on Appropriations,* 95th Cong., 1st Sess.

141. U.S. Congress, Senate Committee on Foreign Relations, *The International Security Assistance and Arms Export Control Act of 1977. Report to Accompany S. 1160,* Report No. 195, 95th Congress, Issued May 16, 1977.

142. U.S. Congress, House, *Prospective Sale of AWACs to Iran: Hearings before the Subcommittee on International Security and Scientific Affairs,* 95th Cong., 1st Sess., June 29–July 21, 1977.

143. *Washington Star,* August 1, 1977; *Washington Post,* July 27, 1977.

144. U.S. Congress, Senate, *International Security Assistance Program, Hearings before the Committee on Foreign Relations on S. 2846,* 95th Cong., 2d Sess., April 25–May 2, 1978; *Foreign Assistance and Related Programs Appropriations for FY 1979, Hearings before the Subcommittee on Foreign Operations on H.R. 12931,* 95th Cong., 2d Sess.; House, *Foreign Assistance Legislation for FY 1979, Hearings before the Committee on International Relations,* 95th Cong., 2d Sess., April 5–May 3, 1978.

145. *Washington Post,* July 24, 1978, p. A-14.

146. U.S. Congress, House Committee on Appropriations, *Foreign Assistance and Related Programs Appropriation Bill, 1979. Report together with Minority and Additional Views to Accompany H.R. 12931,* Report No. 1250, 95th Cong., 2d Sess., June 1, 1978.

147. *Washington Star,* April 11, 1979; *Los Angeles Times,* April 10, 1979.

148. "U.S. Foreign Assistance, Remarks at White House Briefing for Members of Congress, May 19, 1980," *Public Papers of the President: Carter,* pp. 941–44.

149. See U.S. Congress, Senate, *FY 1981 Foreign Assistance Legislation, Hearings before the Committee on Foreign Relations on S. 2423, S. 2422, S. 2588,* 96th Cong., 2d Sess., March 12–April 16, 1980; *Foreign Assistance and Related Programs Appropriation for FY 1981, Hearings before a Subcommittee on H.R. 4473,* 96th Cong., 2d Sess.; House, *Foreign Assistance Legislation for FY 1981, Hearings before the Committee on Foreign Affairs,* 96th Cong., 2d Sess., February 5–March 7, 1980; *Foreign Assistance and Related Programs Appropriation Bill, 1981. Report together with Minority Views to Accompany H.R. 1854.* Report No. 1207, July 29, 1980.

150. "Announcement Concerning a Presidential Directive on United States Conventional Arms Transfer Policy, July 9, 1981," *Public Papers of the President: Reagan, 1981,* pp. 615–617.

151. Pierre, *Global Politics,* pp. 62–63.

152. "Statement on Signing International Security and Foreign Assistance Legislation, December 29, 1981," *Public Papers of the President: Reagan, 1981,* pp. 1202–1204.

153. See U.S. Congress, Senate, *Foreign Assistance Authorization for FY 1982, Hearings before the Committee on Foreign Relations,* 97th Cong.,

1st Sess., March 19–April 22, 1981; House, *Review of U.S. Policy on Military Assistance to Argentina, Hearings before a Subcommittee of the Committee on Foreign Affairs,* 97th Cong., 1st Sess., April 1, 1981; *Foreign Assistance Legislation for FY 1982, Hearings before the Committee on Foreign Affairs,* 97th Cong., 1st Sess., March 13–May 13, 1981.

154. *The Commission on Security and Economic Assistance. A Report to the Secretary of State,* November 1983 (Washington, D.C.: U.S. Department of State, 1983).

3
The Government's Approach to Security Assistance Decisions

Franklin D. Kramer

The conventional wisdom in the national security community is that security assistance is a program in trouble—in 1983 the secretary of state commissioned a high-level panel (the Commission on Security and Economic Assistance) whose mandate was to improve the reception that the security assistance program receives. This chapter seeks to determine the validity of that perception and to analyze the government's approach to security assistance decisions, focusing on executive branch and congressional decisions between 1977 and the present and on the security assistance budget. In part, this chapter is based on interviews with executive branch and congressional participants in the security assistance process.

Introduction to Security Assistance

Security assistance is a term capable of myriad definitions. The U.S. government assists the security of other nations in a variety of ways. Arms are sold to other nations directly by the government and by commercial sources pursuant to government license. Equipment is leased or loaned by the United States to foreign governments. War reserve stocks for wartime use by allies are set aside. Special terms are arranged by the United States to finance some weapons purchases by other countries, and generally recoverable costs of weapons sometimes may be waived by the United States in making sales.

Although these forms of security assistance are not entirely ig-

---

The use of "participants" in this chapter refers to those interviewed in Congress and within the executive branch. To ensure frankness the interviews were done on a not-for-attribution basis.

nored in this study, the emphasis is on monetary assistance, which requires that sums be authorized and appropriated by the Congress. In part, this is because only in making the security assistance budget are both branches of the government equally engaged. On other security assistance matters, the executive may act alone or only subject to congressional veto. Thus, the executive may approve commercial arms sales, waive research and development charges on government-to-government arms sales, and lease or loan equipment, subject only to general statutory strictures set by Congress, which is not involved in case-by-case decisions. (The recent Supreme Court decision against the legislative veto makes it unclear exactly what role the Congress will play in future government-to-government arms sales.) By contrast, the Congress must approve the security assistance budget sent it by the executive.

Four types of assistance comprise the bulk of the security assistance budget—foreign military sales (FMS) credits, grant military aid, economic support funds (ESF), and international military education and training (IMET) funds. (Funds for United Nations peacekeeping operations and special funds, such as for the construction of Israeli airfields in the Negev, are not considered).

Foreign military sales credits are used to lend money to foreign countries to purchase weapons (almost always from the United States). The loans are usually financed by the U.S. government, borrowing money on the open market and lending the money at the market interest rates to foreign countries. These are "guaranteed" loans, although since the obligation is that of the U.S. government, no guarantee is really necessary. Pursuant to statutory requirement, however, the Defense Security Assistance Agency manages a reserve fund that guarantees to the Federal Financing Bank (the agency that asks the Treasury to borrow the funds) repayment of the loan. (Theoretically, loans also could be made by commercial institutions to recipients and guaranteed by the government, but such loans are not often made.) Loans also may be made directly from appropriated funds ("direct loans") with the interest rate determined administratively; generally, the interest rate would be lower than the market rate. Direct loans have rarely been used except the "direct loans" to Israel, and now Egypt, that are forgiven entirely.

Grant military aid is the gift of appropriated funds to purchase weapons from the United States. Economic support funds may be either loans or grants and provide budget support for countries pressed by the burden of maintaining their military. International military education and training are grant funds that provide for the training of foreign military personnel by the U.S. armed forces.

To understand the government's approach to these forms of security assistance, it is necessary to understand the process by which such funds are provided. Preparation of the security assistance budget for any given fiscal year (which runs from October 1 to the following September 30) begins some eighteen months prior to the beginning of the fiscal year. The Office of Management and Budget (OMB) gives the Department of State, as part of whose budget security assistance funds are approved, a "mark," or target, which State is to utilize in shaping the security assistance budget. State, which generally has a good idea of the size of the mark even before it arrives, already will be engaged in the budget development process, having sought from our embassies abroad their estimates of the appropriate size of the security assistance budget for individual countries. The country team figures are reviewed at State by the regional bureaus and then integrated into a first-cut budget by the Bureau of Politico-Military Affairs and the Office of the Undersecretary of State for Security Assistance. The first-cut figures are then further reviewed in an interagency process involving the Department of State, the Department of Defense (DOD), OMB, and, to some extent, the National Security Council (NSC) staff. An agreed figure generally emerges from this process and is reviewed by the secretary of state and frequently the secretary of defense. The figure is then reviewed by the president as part of the fall budget review that establishes the final presidential budget that is sent to Congress.

When the presidential budget arises in the Congress, the budget committees of each house analyze it, using the president's proposal as a basis for preparing a preliminary congressional budget. In establishing that budget, the budget committees receive input from the foreign affairs committees, which must authorize the security assistance budget. Subsequently, in the late spring Congress will pass its first budget resolution, providing both an overall budget and an amount for security assistance. The authorizing committees then pass authorizing legislation and the appropriating committees pass appropriating legislation, the amounts authorized and appropriated supposedly falling within the limits set by the first, and, subsequently, the second budget resolution proposed by the budget committees and voted by the Congress.

While the president's budget provides detailed information for each part of the security assistance budget, the authorizing and appropriating committees generally do not pass line-by-line legislation for each country in the program. Instead, lump sums are authorized and appropriated, except that for grant military assistance and for a few foreign military sales credits (including those that are nominally loans but are actually grants whose repayment is forgiven in advance), for which country-by-country legislation is provided. Once the sums are authorized and appropriated, the executive branch is required to provide a report of how it plans to spend the nonspecifically designated funds. No changes can be made in these plans without giving fifteen-days' notice to Congress (technically, Congress has no veto), and no change can be made in the line-by-line items without formal reprogramming which requires notification of the authorization and appropriations committees, who may deny the request by an affirmative vote. Toward the end of each fiscal year the executive branch will evaluate whether the designated recipients of funds are able to spend them and, if they are not, will allocate such funds to other countries that can.

From fiscal year 1977 through fiscal year 1983, the aggregate value of the programs funded by the security assistance budget (FMS credits, grant aid, ESF, and IMET) has increased substantially from $3.8 billion to $7.8 billion. The growth has been largely accomplished during the last three years, the FY 1981–FY 1983 budget years (although the $3.7 billion one-time funding associated with the peace treaty between Israel and Egypt made FY 1979 the highest single year for the security assistance budget, with a total of $7.9 billion).

The bulk of the growth has been in foreign military sales credits. FMS credit funding has gone from $1.9 billion in FY 1977 to $4.8 billion in FY 1983.

FMS Credits
($ billion)

1977	*1978*	*1979*	*1980*	*1981*	*1982*	*1983*
1.9	2.1	5.7	2.0	3.0	3.8	4.8

The "forgiven" portion of the credits increased from $520 million in FY 1977, which was for Isreal only, to $1.175 billion in FY 1983, of which $750 million was for Israel and $425 million for Egypt.

Economic support funds have significantly grown, from $1.7 billion in FY 1977 to $2.7 billion in FY 1983.

ESF Funds
($ billion)

1977	*1978*	*1979*	*1980*	*1981*	*1982*	*1983*
1.7	2.2	2.0	2.2	2.2	2.6	2.7

Grant military assistance as a result of the military assistance program was about $264 million in FY 1977, dropped to $83 million in FY 1979 and rose to $290 million in FY 1983 (the administration requested approximately $750 million for FY 1984). International military education and training increased from $25 million in FY 1977 to $45 million in FY 1983.

A notable factor about security assistance is that only a very few countries garner the very great portion of the security assistance budget. Only seven countries—Israel, Egypt, Greece, Turkey, Spain, Pakistan, and Korea—received more than $100 million annually in FMS grants from FY 1977 to FY 1983 and only seven—Israel, Egypt, Spain, Portugal, Turkey, El Salvador, and Pakistan—received more than $100 million annually in ESF in FY 1977 to FY 1982.

The foregoing sets forth the formal aspects and the budgetary results for the past seven years of the security assistance program. In the two sections that immediately follow, participants in the process from the executive branch and the Congress provide their view of how the process works and the aims which it is designed to achieve.

The Executive Branch Approach to Security Assistance

As is true of any large organization, the executive branch does not have a monolithic approach to problems, and the views of those interviewed show that the executive's approach to the security assistance program is no exception. As noted above, the major actors within the executive branch are the Departments of State and Defense, OMB, and, occasionally, the White House, through the NSC staff. Each, as the participants' descriptions demonstrate, tends to approach the security assistance budget somewhat differently and there are often divergent views, even within each.

The OMB approach is budgetary—like other programs, security assistance must fit within the president's overall budgetary goals. According to participants, the single most important factor for the OMB in determining how much of the budget to devote to the security assistance program is the size of last year's security assistance budget, which provides the base line according to which the OMB sets its new mark. History is the key for OMB's determination of the mark. The OMB also may consider those events of the past year that affect the desirable amount of security assistance and may make an educated judgment as to what amount Congress will accept. In prior years the OMB tended to build the mark in a fairly sophisticated manner, but more recently, participants suggest, there is a tendency to deal largely with the aggregate number. To some extent, estimates of the degree of congressional acceptability are used to justify limitations on increases. As one participant said, by nature OMB is not looking to expand the program—it is oriented to budget size and domestic politics rather than foreign assistance. The OMB also tends to doubt that Congress will accept substantial increases, and it does not want to allocate a significant portion of increases in the president's budget to a program that will not be approved by the Congress.

By most accounts, the OMB mark is highly significant. Once the OMB mark is established, it is very difficult to raise it without the personal intervention of the secretary of state to the president. One policy participant noted that while secretaries of state tend to care in principle about the level of security assistance, they often tend not to care enough to intervene directly with the president. Another noted that whether the secretary will engage in debate with respect to the OMB mark is critical. It was further suggested that the Reagan secretaries of state had been willing to go to the president for a larger security assistance budget and that the OMB had not been given presidential support to keep this budget item down. Thus, presidential security assistance budgets have increased.

As previously noted, the Department of State has the central role in developing the country components of the security assistance budget. State establishes a preliminary budget that is reviewed during the spring and summer in an interagency review process called the Security Assistance Planning Review Working Group (SAPRWG). In the SAPRWG, DOD and OMB get an opportunity to provide input on a country-by-country basis. Generally, the SAPRWG will decide to increase or maintain program levels, not to decrease them. One participant said that this tendency was only natural: the ultimately proposed administration numbers tend to be read like tea leaves abroad as messages of the direction of U.S. policy. To the extent that no negative changes are made, no issue of adversely changed policy arises.

The SAPRWG's decisions are then sent to the undersecretary of state. The undersecretary of defense for policy may raise some issues with the undersecretary of state, which are generally resolved between the two, leading to an agreed State and Defense program. Traditionally, the security assistance program has not been analyzed vis-à-vis foreign aid provided by the development assistance programs; except for the development of the FY 1984 budget, participants noted that the undersecretary of state was instructed to, and did, provide a budget integrating the two and making trade-offs between them. To some participants, this integrating review amounted to a breakdown of the interagency security assistance budget process because consensually agreed-upon interagency numbers were revised by State—and a single office within State—alone. The degree of which such integration by the undersecretary will continue is unclear. The Agency for International Development (AID) is said to be seriously opposed. How ever the final numbers are reached, the undersecretary's program goes via the secretary of state to OMB and the president as part of the fall budget review, at which time the secretary of state must decide whether to take to the president any differences with the OMB.

Security assistance is obviously a militarily-oriented program, but the executive branch's motivations in providing the assistance go far beyond the military. Many participants tended to emphasize the international political aspects of the program, especially the effect of the program on U.S. relations with the recipient country, one participant noting that international politics are very important in the decisions about large parts of the program. This participant gave Egypt, Israel, and Jordan as good examples. Another participant said that the entire arms transfer business is really a political one. The major decisions are not made on military grounds, but rather are made for domestic and international political reasons. Politics overwhelms the military equation. Still another participant noted that, although international politics drives the program, it is sometimes difficult to make the political argument out loud, which leads to a greater emphasis on the military than otherwise would be the case.

Other participants, however, made a more discriminating case. One participant broke the program down into four motivating categories

1. Base Rights Countries (such as Spain, Philippines, Portugal): in these countries the United States maintains important bases. The assistance is looked upon as an entitlement by the receiving country and as rent by the United States for the facilities. The military needs of the countries tend to be quite limited.

2. Countries with legitimate military needs, but not of substantial importance to the United States except as they provide access to U.S. forces: Morocco, Oman, Kenya, Djibouti, and Honduras were placed in this category. These are countries whose military needs are sufficient to justify the levels that are provided, but without the U.S. special interest in the country, it seems doubtful that we would be at the level we are.

3. Programs which are really military: Korea, Thailand, and Pakistan were placed in this category. Each of these countries faces a

hostile neighbor. We do not want them overrun, and would prefer not to have to intervene. Security assistance is the "ounce of prevention."

4. Highly political: Egypt and Jordan were placed in this category. For these countries, it is possible to justify military requirements, but the point of security assistance is political. The small programs for Latin American and African countries also generally fall within the political category.

Whether all would agree with the countries placed in the categories is uncertain, but the categories themselves—and especialy their political content—get substantial support.

A different participant noted that while nonmilitary factors are important in security assistance, for DOD security assistance presents a serious military program issue. Military establishments are the direct recipients of the security assistance program, and the assistance ultimately provided has to be appropriate from a military point of view. One participant noted that there generally is an ongoing dialogue with recipients of security assistance about their overall military programs, and the money provided by security assistance is utilized to fund all or part of that overall program. Thus, the funds are part of an overall military planning rationale, although not necessarily the one that the U.S. military would choose. If, for example, the army is the most powerful service in the country, the navy will tend to get short shrift regardless of its needs. Nonetheless, for DOD, once a program is decided upon, it is a serious program, military factors weigh heavily, and for reasons of professionalism, if nothing else (and often there is more), it becomes important to carry out the program in a respectable fashion.

As the issue goes higher in DOD, however, a participant noted that the view toward the program becomes more political. Senior people want the program to make military sense, but they also consider more explicitly the other benefits (including international political leverage) that it provides. Another said that the issue of regional balances often gives the program more military weight (if only for perceptual purposes) in the recipient country than the United States might accord the program. A different participant said that while the international political dimension is important, that does not necessarily mean that U.S. policy planners are able to effectuate political goals without taking military realities into account. The quality of military support provides meaningful political advantages, and it is up to the Department of Defense to assure that necessary degree of quality. To be sure, international politics are important. As one person said, "We're not just trying to maintain the security of Egypt which we didn't do for years. We also have larger goals there."

Another participant underscored the political content of the program by noting that, in the end, much of the security assistance budget process is a very large discussion of very little money. Individual country program sums are not large, expecially given the costs of today's weapons. Furthermore, the United States has no equipment set aside in inventory for assistance, so the provision of security assistance generally means that the recipient country is on the U.S. order book to be supplied in three or four years, unless the international political importance of providing the equipment warrants taking it from the U.S. inventory. Because the United States generally does not respond to immediate military needs, the inference is that the international political component of the program is often of greater significance than the military. Another suggested that the program gets the attention that it does and is of such political importance because it is the last hard currency circulating in international relations. The United States lacks the influence it once had, has no large trade or similar programs to buy influence with, and thus security assistance provides a unique governmental opportunity. Another participant agreed, noting that although many countries want U.S. trade or financial assistance, trade largely is provided by private U.S. companies and financial assistance through multilateral organizations, so that the U.S. government largely can trade only in security assistance.

The Congressional Approach to Security Assistance

As with the executive branch, Congress does not consider the security assistance budget in a unitary fashion. Rather, the budget, foreign affairs, and appropriations committees all deal with the security assistance budget.

The first consideration that the House and Senate give the security assistance budget is the number that the authorization committees must provide the budget committees. This budget figure does not seem to be particularly important to the authorizing committees. One participant said that the committee doesn't pay a lot of attention to the budget resolution, and, indeed, the committees usually report the same number as the president's budget. Another noted that the figure that is reported is not very carefully considered in the committee, and there has been no real chance to look at country programs. Unless the number in the president's budget is exceptionally out of line, the committees, in one participant's phrase, "take a look at it and vomit it back."

Whatever the validity of the figure adopted by the budget committees, those interviewed say it does have some effect on the rest of the process. The authorizing committee chairman looks at the bill in the context of the budget, recognizing that the figure that he produces cannot be inconsistent with guidelines from the budget committee without very good reason. Thus, as one person said, throughout the process the chairman is putting pressure on to keep the total down, while the pressures from individual members are often to increase the total figure. It was also suggested that, in tight budget times, the budget figure means more.

Once the authorization process begins, there are differences in the nature of the Senate and House process. The differences are attributed largely to the fewer number of senators, meaning each senator has far more areas of responsibility proportionally than each congressman, and to the absence of the working subcommittee structure for budget purposes in the Senate, the presence of which in the House helps members focus their attention.

According to many participants, the consequence of the myriad demands on a senator's time and the absence of a working subcommittee structure is that Senate staff tend to have greater influence over the budget than their House counterparts, particularly with respect to small country programs. House members, said one participant, are far more informed than senators, simply because of the demands on the latter's time. The use made of the House subcommittees and the fewer areas of responsibility for House members leads to relatively greater member involvement in the smaller, less controversial programs, than in the Senate. While large or controversial programs do get significant senatorial attention, said another, senators generally cannot, and do not, pay "line-item" attention to the entire budget, and staff input sometimes takes on a dimension out of proportion to what the founding fathers intended. Rather than reviewing the entire budget, another participant said, senators often have particular issues that are important to them and so long as they are not fundamental to other senators, the views of the single senator, regardless of party, tends to control.

Participants generally modified the foregoing by saying that there are some senators who carefully review the entire security assistance budget. One person said that an analysis that denigrated the budget review process in the Senate because of an absence of attention to detail by most senators was too simplistic. According to this participant, while there is a tendency not to disturb judgments made in previous years, there is also an annual serious review of the relatively few countries that consume the bulk of the security assistance budget (Israel, Egypt, Turkey, Greece, Pakistan, Spain, and Korea). Those countries who receive less than $100 million annually get less attention unless there is a problem. Even then, some attention is paid, but often there is agreement with the executive branch, and the absence of disagreement tends to look like the absence of attention. As noted above, large or controversial programs get significant, senatorial attention annually.

Another difference between the House and the Senate arises because certain of the House subcommittees appear to some participants to be more liberal than the full committee and because in the full House, there is a substantial block of votes against foreign assistance. Thus, an important role for the House committee chairman is to create a majority for foreign assistance legislation—first in the full committee, then on the floor, given the diverse directions that various parts of the House are moving on security assistance issues.

Once the authorizing committees begin the review process, those interviewed seemed to agree that there is substantial congruence on the factors that the Senate and the House consider. Virtually all agree that the previous year's figure serves as a base, and new or significantly increased programs get more scrutiny than existing programs. The assumption is that the old figures are satisfactory, and that only the new figures deserve review. As in all ongoing programs, said one person, one tends to presuppose that judgments made before are okay. Similarly, another said, one looks at total figures in comparison with last year to see what the administration is trying to do. On the House side, consideration starts at the subcommittee level and, while the proposed figures are compared to the prior year's figures, there is no look at the total security assistance figures until the full committee consideration.

The committees proceed through hearings in a process that tends to be somewhat adversarial between the executive branch and the Congress. There are differences of view as to whether that is good or bad, one participant stating that such a relationship is fundamental to democracy but another noting that there was an absence of forthrightness on the part of the executive branch. A third person added that certain people in the Congress tended not to believe anything the executive branch said. A somewhat widespread reaction was that, with the exception of a few executive branch witnesses, if the right question is not asked, the full answer isn't given. Another said that the executive branch is very willing to supply whatever information members sought, but the executive provides that information only to the extent Congress requests it, and Congress may not always ask for what was relevant.

Whether Congress receives sufficient information is open to dispute. One participant noted that the information flow is limited. Another noted, however, that members in each House may have more information than they usefully can absorb, especially because Congress receives a great deal of competing information. Thus, information from the executive branch is only one source; other sources include the Government Accounting Office (GAO), Library of Congress, think tanks and, especially, pressure groups. One person noted that it can be difficult for members to distinguish between pressure groups with substantial memberships and those with limited followings but articulate, energetic spokesmen. Pressure groups have all learned that they get more attention if they put their message in writing and even more if they put it on a letterhead.

When the issues are addressed, the two houses again tend to have the same general approaches. Though security assistance includes military assistance and economic assistance, participants said that the Congress tends to look at the money spent as paying for international political goals first and only accomplishing military or economic ends second. This was not an objection to the program—one participant said, members of Congress are professional politicians and understand the value of political arrangements: spending money to obtain "warm fuzzies" is accepted. Another agreed that the point of the money is for international political leverage, and a third stated that the reality of money is strictly political. This is not to say that participants felt that there were no military or economic rationales for security assistance. Rather, military and economic considerations were secondary to, as one participant said, the overwhelming political nature of the money.

According to participants, Congress' approach to security assistance as primarily political tends to increase skepticism concerning some executive branch testimony. As one participant said, when you and the witness know that the point of foreign military sales credits is political, you lose confidence in the information you're getting from that witness when he insists on a military rationale for the money being supplied. Referring to one case, a participant said that the witness had no sound ideas as to the details of how the assistance would actually aid, and had been less than candid as to the effectiveness and timeliness of the assistance. Another said that the executive branch often defends its figures as if those were the only ones that could be drawn, providing a military rationale that Congress knows could be altered. It weakens the credibility of the executive branch to defend security assistance on solely military and economic grounds when no one believes that. In the phrase of one participant, military assistance to most recipients is analogous to giving diamonds to a prostitute; the equipment purchased is useful to the recipient as a prestige symbol, but does not create much military capability.

In discussing the five countries—Israel, Egypt, Turkey, Greece, and Spain—that get the bulk of security assistance, the international political aspects of security assistance were emphasized by participants. Aid to Spain was seen as a quid pro quo for the use of bases in Spain by the United States. Security assistance for Egypt was also viewed as being clearly for international political purposes. Many observers believed that the Egyptians did not need the current level of security assistance. Rather, they believed, as one said, that the main reason that the United States is so involved with Egypt is to show the Arab world that the United States is not interested only in Israel, but would also be helpful to a country that participated in the Middle East peace process. One participant ascribed a similar view to President Sadat, saying that Sadat said that if the funds to Israel were cut, then the Egyptians would be willing to forego the assistance since they didn't need it. Another ascribed the high Egyptian levels partly to supporters of Israel who now find it desirable to show broad-mindedness about security assistance to Egypt, rather than having an Israel-only coloration.

Egypt was illustrative, according to several, of the phenomenon of security assistance recipients lobbying the Congress, sometimes successfully. It was noted that Egypt had refused to sign a facilities access agreement with the United States and it was questioned whether, in a crisis, Egypt would be of assistance to the United States. Nonetheless, as one participant suggested, President Hosni Mubarak visits the Congress when in Washington, meets with congressional delegations in Egypt, and continuously stresses how good a friend of the United States the Egyptians are and how important security assistance is to Egypt. Such statements produce results in terms of more security assistance. Mubarak's approach to Congress is illustrative; numerous foreign leaders have taken to lobbying Congress directly, and in several cases they have gotten an uneasy Congress to go along with a proposed program. Foreign leaders can be the best advocates of security assistance, said one participant—if they do a good job. A bad job, by implication, can ensure defeat of a questionable proposal.

On Israel, there was widespread agreement that Israel's military situation dictates a large Israeli security assistance program. There were differences on just how large a program this meant, and, therefore, differences of view on whether the program served political as well as military ends. Many said that, from a military standpoint, the Israeli program is at an appropriate level from Congress's point of view, and some emphasized that Congress had increased the Israeli security assistance program over administration requests. Another said that while some in the Congress have a vague feeling that Israel's levels are higher than militarily necessary, if those who have such a feeling went into the issue to the extent done by Committee members and staff, the military justification for the Israeli numbers would appear. According to this person, the votes on security assistance for Israel are better considered and have more depth than observers of the Congress tend to believe.

Others, however, expressed less military-oriented justifications for the Israeli program. When voting for security assistance for Israel, the feeling is that Congress is helping Israel's security only in an abstract way; they are providing budget support for Israel rather than needed military items, and they are providing it in response to political pressures in the United States rather than in response to security needs. Others said that if there were a secret ballot, the results would be different, that only domestic constraints precluded lowering somewhat the amount of money Israel received. Even among those expressing this view, however, no one doubts that Israel has real security needs or that the United States should meet them. The differences thus seemed marginal, rather than fundamental.

Turkey was a country to which Congress seemed willing to extend aid because it is a NATO ally directly facing the Soviet Union. Turkey illustrated the fact that Soviet containment can be a major motivating factor for the Congress and that military aid as military aid can be seen as important. Turkey appears to be one of the few countries for which this approach is generally accepted as the real motivating factor for assistance.

Security assistance to Greece was understood by the participants in two different ways in Congress. Some emphasized the domestic political context, noting that some members of Congress are particularly interested and that gives the program a push. Additionally, and importantly, it is also the case, as one person put it, that aid to Greece is a vital voting issue for certain constituencies. Those persons will know how the member voted on the issue and that determined whether they would vote for the member. Since there was no countervailing force, it was easy for members to vote for aid to Greece. On the other hand, others viewed aid to Greece in terms of the regional situations—the Turks and the Greeks count the balance between them as part of their security equation, even if we did not, and U.S. interests are better served when it did as well. While the current ratio of Turkish–Greek aid is not analytically immutable, changing it would be read as a significant change in policy that would be hard to justify.

Finally, beyond the issues noted above, there are several others that motivate Congress, not all pointing in the same direction. Several participants said that Congress was concerned about the military and economic aid balance and questioned whether the United States overemphasized military aid. Others suggested that Congress was still concerned about giving the executive branch too much flexibility. The special defense acquisition fund had difficulty in getting through Congress because Congress did not want to provide a "slush fund" to the executive branch. On the other hand, many members want to support the president, holding the view that he is ultimately responsible for foreign policy. There was a general feeling that the United States was in a difficult period and that the international political leverage obtained by security assistance was useful. One participant added that it was sometimes important to support the president even in his mistakes.

While the president has great influence on the security assistance budget, so do constituents, and constituent involvement appears to have broadened. As an example, it was noted that human rights and nuclear nonproliferation issues have begun to cause an activist position among various church hierarchies, and professional politicians do not forget that their consituency will respond to such views. Other groups, though not as broadly based, have become even more active, some in favor and some against security assistance.

To the extent that any large group will influence a member of Congress, large groups active on security assistance will get a hearing. No one suggested that domestic groups dominated the process. An important aspect of the influence of domestic groups was noted by one participant who, in views shared by others, said the major thing that the so-called domestic lobbies do is present counterarguments to the executive branch. This keeps the executive branch from having a free rein in making policy. The domestic constituency will not win, however, if it does not have good arguments and is not able to persuade a lot of people that its views are consistent with U.S. interests.

Results of the Interaction between the Executive and Congress

The result of the executive and congressional process, of course, is the actual security assistance budget. Scrutiny of the process allows several conclusions to be drawn.

The first conclusion is that security assistance is a highly successful congressional program. As previously noted, the size of the program has very substantially increased in recent years. FMS credits have more than doubled since FY 1977. In the same time period, ESF has increased by about 50 percent and IMET by about 80 percent. Even MAP has modestly increased and is more than three times the figure of FY 1979. Moreover, when forgiven credits are added to the MAP program, the growth in forgiven loans for Israel and Egypt means that grants have grown 190 percent. The proposals for FY 1984 ($5.4 billion for FMS credits, $2.7 billion for ESF, $701 million for MAP, and $57 million for IMET) increase this trend and, if enacted, would result in total increases since FY 1977 of 270 percent for FMS credits, 160 percent for ESF, 230 percent for IMET, and 265 percent for MAP. It is fair to note that a significant portion of this increase is inflationary. If the administration's FY 1984 budget is enacted, however, much of the security assistance budget will have increased more than 210 percent since FY 1977, which is the amount of increase for the entire federal budget as a whole. In short, an important conclusion about the security assistance program is that it is hardly a program in overall difficulty.

Indeed, it seems fair to say that the Congress provides little significant check on overall executive branch plans. Thus, in terms of overall program authority, the authorizing committees in seven years provided more than the executive asked in FMS credits four times and virtually the same once. In the other two years, the differences were less than 10 percent of the requested program size. The appropriations committees tended to provide fewer FMS credits than requested, but the aggregate program financed by appropriations was on one occasion more than requested, and in the other six years appropriations funded a program 10 percent less than requested.

Similarly, both the authorizing and appropriations committees provided as much or more ESF as requested by the executive: the authorizing committees exceeding the request in three of seven years, virtually identical in two other years, and less than 10 percent short in the remaining two; the appropriations committees exceeding the request in two of seven years, in two others only 1 percent less and in the other three only 8 percent less. Finally, for the four-year period between FY 1979 and FY 1982, the executive branch proposed to the Congress thirty-one security-assistance-related legislative initiatives of which twenty-six were enacted in whole or in part.

To be sure, Congress does have an impact on the FMS program, but it is less on the overall program size (as the figures discussed above indicate) than on specific decisions within the program. Indeed, the congressional impact on the overall security assistance budget is somewhat more limited than might be expected. It is hardly a surprise, whenever a full-scale review is conducted of any program that has required difficult judgment calls, that the reviewer will find places to differ from the judgments made. Because Congress generally is not engaged in the making of the executive branch budget, it feels free to require rehearsal of the reasons for the judgments made and to reverse decisions with which it disagrees. That the Congress changes the budget as little as it does is more surprising than the extent to which the budget is changed.

The second conclusion is that the security assistance program is presented in a fashion that maximizes diplomatic problems and exacerbates the negative effect of the congressional review process. Tables 3–1 and 3–2 set forth the country-by-country FMS credits request of the executive branch and the actual amounts approved for each country after the completed congressional process for FY 1982 and FY 1983. As the tables indicate, most of the individual country amounts do not differ much from the requested amounts. As noted above, the FMS credit program fares fairly well in the Congress.

There is an obvious observation which may be drawn from the chart. The observation derives from the fact that the executive branch request is public knowledge, well-known to each potential country recipient, and from the fact that almost every country has had a "change" from the proposed to the actual figures. As noted above by one participant, changes in figures are read like tea leaves abroad, and the changes from the proposed to the actual budget will cause each recipient country to peer into the tea leaves and try to fathom why its funding was altered during the process, how it fared vis-à-vis other countries, and whether those differences are significant. In

Table 3–1
FY 1982 Foreign Military Sales Financing Program
(millions of dollars)

	President's Budget (Mar. 81)	*Congressional Earmarks*[a]	*Section 653 Levels*[b]	*Actual Levels*[c]
East Asia and Pacific	355.5		328.50	340.70
Indonesia	45.0		40.00	40.00
Korea	167.0		166.00	166.00
Malaysia	12.5		10.00	10.00
Philippines	50.0		50.00	50.00
Thailand	80.0		62.50	74.70
Near East and South Asia	2545.0		2517.00	2531.90
Egypt	900.0	200.00	900.00	900.00
Israel	1400.0	1400.00	1400.00	1400.00
Jordan	50.0		50.00	54.90
Lebanon	15.0		10.00	10.00
Morocco	30.0		30.00	30.00
Oman	40.0		30.00	30.00
Pakistan	—		—	—
Sri Lanka	—		2.00	2.00
Tunisia	95.0		85.00	95.00
Yemen	15.0		10.00	10.00
Europe	870.0		793.00	793.00
Greece	260.0	280.00	280.00	280.00
Portugal	60.0		45.00	45.00
Spain	150.0		125.00	125.00
Turkey	400.0		343.00	343.00
Africa	202.9	50.00	132.60	153.10
American Republics	81.5		62.40	64.80
Worldwide Total	4054.9	1930.00	3833.50	3883.50

[a]"Congressional earmarks" are the amounts called for by committee reports and authorization and appropriations acts. Where the appropriated amount was less than the other earmarks, this lower amount is listed. The $50 million listed for Africa was earmarked for the Sudan.

[b]"Section 653 levels" are the amounts that the president notified Congress would be allocated to specific countries within the total of $3,833.5 million in FMSCR that Congress initially authorized and appropriated for FY 1982.

[c]"Actual levels" are the amounts actually allocated to specific countries following later congressional approval of an FY 1982 supplemental of $50 million for the Sudan.

Table 3–2
FY 1983 Foreign Military Sales Financing Program
(millions of dollars)

	President's Budget (Jan. 82)	*Congressional Earmarks*[a]	*CRA Planning Levels*[b]	*Total with Supplemental*[c]
East Asia and Pacific	413.5		271.00	388.50
Indonesia	50.0		20.00	50.00
Korea	210.0		140.00	210.00
Malaysia	12.5		4.00	12.50
Philippines	50.0		50.00	50.00
Thailand	91.0		57.00	66.00
Near East and South Asia	3660.0		3446.00	3705.00
Egypt	1300.0	1325.00	1325.00	1300.00
Israel	1700.0	1700.00	1700.00	1700.00
Jordan	75.0		40.00	75.00
Lebanon	15.0	10.00	10.00	15.00
Morocco	100.0	75.00	75.00	100.00
Oman	40.0		30.00	40.00
Pakistan	275.0		200.00	275.00
Sri Lanka	—		—	—
Tunisia	140.0		62.00	105.00
Yemen	15.0		4.00	10.00
Europe	1235.0		1022.50	1087.50
Greece	280.0	280.00	280.00	280.00
Portugal	90.0	52.50	52.50	52.50
Spain	400.0	400.00	400.00	400.00
Turkey	465.0	290.00	290.00	355.00
Africa	234.0		33.70	87.00
American Republics	125.3		39.80	70.00
Worldwide Total	5667.8	4132.50	4813.00	5338.00

[a]"Congressional earmarks" are the amounts called for by committee reports and authorization and appropriations acts. Where the appropriated amount was less than the other earmarks, this lower amount is listed.

[b]"CRA planning levels" are the amounts that the president notified Congress would be allocated to specific countries within the total of $4,813 million available under Continuing Resolution Authority.

[c]The FY 1983 supplemental is still under consideration by Congress.

short, even though the congressional process was highly favorable to the executive branch, the minor alterations caused by congressional action combined with the fact that those alterations are apparent to all means that the executive will have to undertake some substantial amount of diplomacy to explain the results. In such instances, the executive will be on the defensive, facing a disappointed recipient. Whether any other "objectively" successful program could cause the executive so much difficulty seems unlikely. Such a problem may help explain why the executive branch conceives of the program as needing greater support, when, in fact, security assistance gets a significantly positive response from the Congress.

Tables 3–1 and 3–2 also show the FY 1982 and FY 1983 congressional treatment of "earmarked" FMS credit countries. Only four countries—Israel, Egypt, Greece, and the Sudan—were earmarked in FY 1982. The earmarked amounts were equivalent or greater than the executive branch's requests. In FY 1983 eight countries were earmarked, with one getting more than the executive requested, three the same, and four less than requested. To some extent, however, the practice of earmarking may exacerbate the problems caused by the presentation of the security assistance budget to the Congress.

To the extent that Congress earmarks funds for particular countries, any shortfall in funds proportionally greater than the ratio of the earmarked to the requested amount—whether from a decrease in overall program level or an increase in the earmarked country program not matched by an overall increase in the program—will fall heaviest on other countries. During most of the FY 1977 to FY 1983 period, the effect of earmarked countries on other country programs was not significant. Generally, only a few countries were earmarked and in the one year (FY 1981) when several countries were earmarked, Congress also increased the overall program beyond the executive request so that there was not a shortfall.

In FY 1983, however, earmarking presented a problem to the executive in terms of dealing with non-earmarked countries, because eight countries were earmarked, five (Israel, Egypt, Spain, Turkey, and Greece) had substantial programs, and the overall FMS program was less than the executive requested. Once the five large earmarked programs were set aside, the shortfall had to be made up among smaller countries that suffered a proportionally greater effect. To be sure, the executive's ability to establish priorities allows it to place the brunt of a shortfall on the less important countries. Nonetheless, a disproportionate decrease in less immediately significant countries can cause diplomatic difficulties for the United States. In FY 1983 the non-earmarked countries suffered a decline from the proposed amounts of $1.3 billion to $781 million, a reduction of about 40 percent.

The third conclusion is that executive and congressional differences in the security assistance budget reflect policy differences rather than differences in attitude toward security assistance. Executive inability to obtain the security assistance budget that it desires generally reflects policy differences with Congress, rather than differences in attitudes toward security assistance per se. Congress has had no hesitation in generally granting the executive what it requested, as the chronicled growth of the security assistance budget reflects. Indeed, Congress has sometimes offered more than requested.

With the exception of the FY 1983 "earmarking problem," the major executive failures or difficulties have come in those controversial programs where significant policy questions have been at issue. A simple listing makes this clear:

resumption of security assistance to Turkey;

maintenance of the 7:10 Greek to Turkish ratio;

aid to Pakistan; and

aid to El Salvador.

In none of these cases were (or are) the differences attributable to differences in attitudes toward security assistance in general. Rather, congressional policy judgments simply differ from executive judgments.

Similarly, the non-country-oriented executive and congressional disputes largely have reflected differing policy judgments, rather than different attitudes toward security assistance. The most notable congressional alteration in the FY 1982 budget, for example, was the elimination of "direct" credits, funds for loans that would be made at lower rates than the ordinary guaranteed loan. But the decreases in direct credits were offset by increases in guaranteed credits, hardly a demonstration of unwillingness to provide security assistance. Similarly, the long-standing congressional refusal to provide, for a long time any, and even now, a large special defense acquisition fund (which would allow the executive to respond quickly to security assistance needs without the necessity of drawing down equipment from U.S. forces) tends to reflect a mistrust of how the executive will use the fund rather than whether it might be abstractly desirable. On the other hand, repetition of the FY 1983 earmarking problem would demonstrate that Congress did have difficulty in ensuring that the size of the security assistance budget is enough to meet the needs of both earmarked and other security assistance recipients.

The fourth conclusion is that substance, not process, is important. The implication of the preceding is that the process of providing security assistance largely has not significantly affected results. There appear, however, to be three caveats to this conclusion:

1. Since the OMB mark generally provides the contours of the overall debate, the most significant time for contributions to the process is prior to the establishment of that mark.

2. As noted, earmarking combined with reductions in program size can affect lower priority countries.

3. To the extent Congress differs from the executive, that difference often reflects the broader congressional information-gathering processes and the sometimes limited credence that the executive receives. On this latter point, there is, as noted, a feeling in the Congress that the executive is often less than fully candid, frequently not providing all relevant information unless specifically requested. Because Congress also receives information—often at odds with executive branch information—from many sources, implicit in this suggestion is a downgrading of the persuasive value of the executive branch's information.

A corollary of the foregoing is that Congress is unlikely to be disposed to allow the executive greater flexibility over security assistance. To be sure, the executive has some good arguments for such additional flexibility. When a budget is made up eighteen months (and now, with two-year authorizations, thirty months) in advance of the fiscal year, the executive can hardly anticipate all contingencies. On the other hand, providing greater flexibility would reduce Congress' power—and few institutions easily accept such reductions. More important, in circumstances such as now exist, where the executive branch is perceived by the Congress as not wholly candid, and periodically not correct, it seems unlikely that Congress will be willing to accede to greater executive flexibility that would allow the executive to act without congressional control.

The final conclusion is that security assistance often cannot be defended primarily on military grounds. As noted above, both the Congress and many within the executive branch tend to perceive the security assistance program as meeting U.S. international political objectives. The reality is the same: the money does appear far more to achieve these goals for the United States than to provide military assistance for its own sake, so long as "political" is understood to encompass those circumstances not involving direct military threats to the recipient country that are of significant consequence to the United States. Review of the largest proposals for increases or for the start-ups of new programs over the past six years generally confirms this conclusion.

Israel and Egypt consume the largest share of the increases in the budget, with Egypt receiving nothing as late as FY 1978, as compared to $1.3 billion in 1983. Israel, which received $1 billion in FY 1977, received $1.4 billion in FY 1983. While Israel has unquestioned security needs, the threat to Egypt clearly lessened after the peace treaty with Israel was signed. The ever-increasing money can be justified by the decrepit nature of Egyptian equipment, the desirability of demonstrating that the United States will reward an Arab friend, the value of maintaining the military's loyalty, and the value of U.S. access to Egyptian facilities. None of these factors involves a direct military threat to U.S. or Egyptian interests.

A second group of countries receiving substantial increases or beginning new programs in this period included Morocco, Oman, and Somalia. Each of these countries has agreed to provide U.S. forces with access to its facilities in the event of a crisis in Southwest Asia. After each such agreement, each country received a new FMS credit program or a significant increase. That the country's military requirements were not paramount with the United States is suggested by our refusal to provide military aid to Somalia when it was directly threatened by Ethiopia in 1978 or our refusal to increase Moroccan aid when its war against the Polisario was going much worse than it was in 1982 (when the increase was proposed). A similar point might be made about Spain, which trebled its FMS credits through hard bargaining over its bases agreement with the United States, not because the military threat to Spain or the United States had increased.

A third group of countries might be the "reward for transition to democracy" countries. The Dominican Republic, Ecuador, and Honduras fall in this category, as does Jamaica which, if always a democracy, is now a more congenial one. Each of these countries has begun new programs, while the military threat to each (Honduras aside) has not worsened. Honduras has utilized the funds to gain better control of its borders and here it is fair to say a military and a political rationale coincided.

A fourth category of countries might be called the "staying in touch with Africa" group. Botswana, Cameroon, Niger, Rwanda, Liberia, and Senegal all received new or substantially increased FMS credits in FY 1982 with no change in the threat situation for the

United States or for them. All had received ESF funds for years; arguably the FMS credits will be more seductive persuaders.

A fifth group of countries are those for whom the regional military balance has changed negatively. Greece falls in this category, at least when one views the regional balance through Greek eyes. Tunisia likewise can be included because it has been threatened by Libya; and the Sudan can be included for the same reason. While each of the countries has legitimate security concerns, aid to each also serves important U.S. political considerations. Aid to Greece seeks not only to improve Greek military capabilities, but to avoid an excessive political tilt to Turkey, to enhance U.S.–Greek relations, and to encourage Greece to remain part of the NATO alliance. The Sudan is important to the U.S. in substantial part because of U.S.–Egyptian relations and the importance of the Sudan to the Egyptian strategic considerations. Aid to Tunisia is a visible response to Libya.

Finally, there are those countries whose immediate military circumstance is of significant military import to the U.S. and who face a substantial threat. Turkey falls in the first category for NATO and Southwest Asian reasons. Arguably, Pakistan does also. Pakistan, however, may illustrate how international political motives are often coincident with military ones. The United States clearly does not want Pakistan to accommodate the USSR in light of the latter's presence in Afghanistan, and the Pakistanis face a far greater regional threat than before. Whether the provision of FMS credits is a spine stiffener or a response to the threat may depend on the eye of the beholder.

To say that international political considerations interact with or sometimes dominate military considerations in the provision of security assistance is not to say that such considerations are illegitimate. Utilizing military assistance as a means to an end—be it obtaining needed access to support U.S. contingency plans or orienting a country more toward the United States—often will be a highly appropriate use of the program. Such programs, however, cannot be defended solely on military grounds.

4
The Domestic Constituencies of the Security Assistance Program

Robert B. Mahoney, Jr. and *David L. Wallace*

This chapter examines two domestic constituencies for the security assistance program—the general public and interest groups.

Recent surveys sponsored by the Chicago Council on Foreign Relations are reviewed to show how both the public at large and the leaders of U.S. institutions (labor, business, etc.) evaluate economic and military assistance programs and to outline how these evaluations fit within these publics' overall evaluations of foreign policy concerns. Emphasis is given to the post-Vietnam breakdown in consensus among likely opinion leaders concerning national foreign policy objectives.

Assessment of interest groups as constituencies for the security assistance programs, our second focus, centers on three issues:

Which organizations attempt to influence security assistance policy, and for what reasons?

What resources and mechanisms can these groups employ in their attempts to influence the program?

How have these groups attempted to use these resources to influence recent policies?

The chapter closes with recommendations for improving the development and execution of U.S. security assistance programs.

Our purpose is to show how disparate groups assess and interact with the security assistance program. As a consequence, no single theme runs throughout the chapter. Most attention is devoted to providing basic information about constituencies' evaluations of, and interactions with, the program.

Some general patterns of note do, however, emerge concerning support for the security assistance program and the more general range of foreign policy concerns within which security assistance policy operates.

Throughout this assessment, security assistance emerges as the political equivalent of an orphan. There is little support for the program among the public at large. More backing is evident among U.S. leaders. In the post-Vietnam era, however, these leaders are no longer in agreement concerning the goals of U.S. foreign policy or the standards by which programs should be assessed. Only one of the three groups of opinion leaders identified—those who continue to accept the norms of Cold War internationalism—are likely to be highly receptive to the rationales usually presented in support of the program.

Similarly, few groups are interested in the security assistance program in its entirety. Instead, they focus on portions of the program. Their activities often involve the potential use of security assistance programs as a means through which other facets of foreign policy can be affected, rather than reflecting an interest in security assistance, per se.

The absence of consensus concerning foreign policy objectives found among U.S. leaders is also evident in the divergent world views/strategic assessments that both constituencies and members of government use in their deliberations concerning security assistance programs. Differences seldom involve security assistance, narrowly defined. Instead, they are associated with divergent maps of the problems to be addressed, with each map outlining a different course for security assistance and other policies. Security assistance programs figure as only one element on these maps, and not necessarily as the most prominent terrain feature.

Given these divergences, and the reality of increased congressional (and, through Congress, interest group) participation in the development of the program, recommendations for improving the formulation and execution of security assistance policy are developed. Emphasis is given to changes that would increase nonexecutive branch participants' involvement in the formulation of the program and new approaches that would increase the quantity and caliber of information available to these partners in the policy development process.

The Public Constituency

Introduction

The general public is the most diffuse of the constituencies involved in security assistance policy. It is tempting to discount the importance of public views because the public tends to be relatively uninformed concerning current and prospective security assistance programs, giving much greater attention to domestic policy concerns, particularly the economy.[1] Linkages between specific decisions made by elected leaders and public opinion are difficult to identify. Counterbalancing this temptation is a growing body of evidence that shows that at least some congruences exist between public views as captured in opinion polls and the course of national policy, particularly when the two are compared over time.[2]

Elections are the most obvious of the factors that might account for the correlations between public views and foreign and defense policies. Although few, if any, elections are determined by the security assistance policies of the contenders, defense policy is one of the factors considered by the electorate, and the defense policy positions of candidates, while seldom likely to be determining factors, can enter into the electorate's calculations, particularly at the presidential level. Security assistance stances can figure in these assessments. Security aid programs can also be affected by other defense policy positions, such as levels of defense spending, which affect the availability of funds for these programs.

The competitive character of many U.S. elections, particularly at the presidential and senatorial levels, reinforces this point. A 55 percent tally in these contests is a landslide. Hence, candidates may be loath to alienate even a small fraction of their potential electoral margin, and the 1 percent of the electorate that is seriously concerned with providing security assistance to a given country may be 50 percent of a candidate's margin.

Public views can also have effects by helping to define the boundaries of the national policy agenda. In any democracy a menu of politically accceptable policy options exists. Candidates who select items that are not on the menu are likely to encounter problems. For example, arguing strictly on the basis of geopolitical or balance of power criteria, a reasonable case can be made for U.S. initiatives to improve relations with Cuba and the Democratic Republic of Vietnam so as to reduce both nations' dependence on the Soviet Union (past U.S. policies toward Yugoslavia provide a precedent). It takes little imagination to conjecture the criticism and damaging electoral consequences that this position might have drawn had it been proposed by President Carter in either 1976 or 1980.

The End of Consensus

From the Korean War through the early stages of U.S. involvement in Vietnam, there was significant consensus among policymakers and the public at large on the goals of U.S. foreign policy. While emphases differed and a minority of isolationists remained, there was general agreement concerning the goal of containment and the principal means to achieve this objective—the forward presence of U.S. forces as a deterrent in the most critical theaters, such as in Europe, and the provision of military assistance to friendly nations throughout the world.

The fall of Vietnam appears to have shattered this consensus. Subsequently, efforts were undertaken to assess the impact of the war on the foreign policy views of U.S. opinion leaders.[3] To identify these leaders, a sample was taken from *Who's Who in America*. This sample was mailed a survey questionnaire. Return rates were unusually good for this type of sample—2,282 of 4,290 respondents returned the lengthy form. These answers provide the most detailed information available concerning the impact of the war on United States opinion leaders' views.

Selecting items from this survey that bear on security assistance are presented in table 4–1. An immediately striking point is the lack of consensus concerning the problem to be addressed by U.S. national security policy in the Third World. A majority of respondents attributed revolutionary forces in the Third World to local factors rather than to Soviet or Chinese activities, the rationale often proposed by administrations in support of security assistance programs.

While the U.S. public has generally been more supportive of economic than military assistance, leaders split evenly on the related question of whether the United States should provide economic aid even at the cost of higher domestic prices, with a slight majority (51 percent) opposing this sacrifice while 48 percent were willing to accept it.[4]

A less even division is evident in responses to the next item, with the minority—37 percent—agreeing that more national attention should be focused on domestic concerns and 62 percent opposing the proposition.

The respondents split evenly on the question of whether the conduct of U.S. foreign policy has relied excessively on military advice, with 49 percent in agreement with the statement and 48 percent opposed. This has potential bearing on public's support for the use of military instruments, such as security assistance, in foreign policy and on its willingness to accept arguments made by Department of Defense advocates of such programs.

In the same vein, just under two-thirds of the opinion leaders agreed with the proposition that presidents have been given too much latitude to define the nation's interests. It is not at all difficult to relate this mid-1970s view to concurrent developments in security

Table 4–1
Selected Foreign Policy Views of U.S. Leaders

Question	*Strongly Agree*	*Agree Somewhat*	*Disagree Somewhat*	*Strongly Disagree*	*No Opinion*
Revolutionary forces in "Third World" countries are usually nationalistic rather than controlled by the USSR or China.	22%	39%	22%	12%	5%
The U.S. should give economic aid to poor countries even if it means higher prices at home.	11	37	32	19	1
We shouldn't think so much in international terms but concentrate more on our own national problems.	11	26	29	33	1
The conduct of U.S. foreign affairs relies excessively on military advice.	20	29	30	18	3
Americans have relied too much on presidents to define the national interest.	26	37	26	9	2
Military aid programs will eventually draw the U.S. into unnecessary wars.	10	31	39	17	3

Source: Adapted from Ole R. Holsti and James N. Rosenau (eds.), *Change in the International System* (Boulder: Westview Press, 1980), pp. 274–279.

assistance policy in which Congress assumed its present role as a more active partner in the formulation of security assistance programs.

Finally, turning to security assistance a significant pattern is evident. The question posed is provocative: "military aid programs will eventually draw the United States into unnecessary wars." This type of assertive wording often dissuades affirmative responses. Here, however, fully 41 percent of the opinion leaders surveyed agreed with the proposition, which does not augur favorably for their support of any security assistance programs.

The relevance of these results goes beyond this survey. Examining patterns that emerge from the responses to the survey, Holsti and Rosenau came to a conclusion that directly bears on current security assistance policy. Based on a careful statistical analysis of the responses, they concluded that U.S. opinion leaders can be divided into three separate groups:

> those that accept the Cold War axioms (with their emphasis on containment of the Soviet Union) that predominated in United States foreign policy deliberations from Korea through Vietnam;
>
> post-Cold War internationalists who reject many of the assumptions that went into containment but still see a need for active U.S. involvement overseas, with emphasis on development assistance and other nonmilitary policy instruments; and
>
> post-Cold War semi-isolationists or nationalists who place emphasis on reducing U.S. involvement in foreign affairs, believe that the United States relies excessively on military policy instruments in its foreign policy and tht the president has had too much latitude in establishing national interests, and are skeptical regarding the benefits of military assistance.

These belief systems are not presented as monolithic ideologies. Instead, they are three, largely mutally exclusive, modal tendencies found among U.S. opinion leaders in the post-Vietnam period.

Analysis by age groups revealed no consistent patterns. It is not simply that the Vietnam generation rejects the axioms of Cold War containment policy. The problem, rather, is a broad-based distribution of all age groups into these three categories. Vietnam appears to have changed the U.S. public's mind, but in markedly different ways.

Of considerable current significance is a conclusion reached by Holsti and Rosenau in their comparison of occupational groups.

Comparing patterns of responses within and between the principal occupations represented in their sample, Holsti and Rosenau found a strong profile of similarity within groups and differences between them. For example, military officers were, with the exception of a few items, more supportive on the average of the principles of cold War containment than were labor union officials.

In the specific case of military assistance efforts, a clear-cut pattern was found, with the occupational groups listed below in descending order of support for U.S. security assistance programs:

(Most supportive)	military officers
	foreign service officers
	business executives
	lawyers
	public officials
	media leaders
	educators
	clergy
(Least supportive)	labor union officials

Two implications for current security assistance programs are evident. First, to the extent that these patterns persist (and Holsti and Rosenau's research suggests that they will), there is no broad-based constituency for security assistance or any other facet of foreign policy. Instead, there are three systems of belief operating in the minds of opinion leaders, only one of which is consistent with the containment policy that has prompted—and continues to prompt—many facets of U.S. security assistance policy. In effect (to anticipate an argument that will be developed at greater length below), adherents of the three tendencies are using different "scripts" to guide their assessments of security assistance issues.

Second, a moral is apparent. The military and foreign service officers involved in formulating arms transfer plans should not be surprised to find themselves in agreement, because the average positions in their two groups are quite close, particularly on this issue. Their views, however, are not necessarily those of elected officials, the media, labor union leaders, and other categories of leaders, who tend to be less supportive of military assistance programs and the rationales that are commonly presented in their support.

Selected Public Views

Security assistance policy is intended to function as one element in an ensemble of U.S. foreign and military policies. In this regard, several aspects of public views are of significance. The first involves the public's perceptions of threats to U.S. national interests on the assumption that perceived threats help to define requirements for security aid programs and the relative importance of different programs.

A clear pattern stands out in recent poll data.[5] By a considerable margin, the U.S. public defines the Soviet Union as the primary threat to U.S. security. Other nations are also of concern, such as Libya and Cuba, but the USSR is seen as predominant concern. This leads to the suggestion that military assistance policies will be most difficult to justify to the public when there is no obvious Soviet involvement in the national security situation being addressed. Attempts to use security assistance to foster regional balances can draw little support from this pattern of views unless Soviet involvement is also perceived.

Another set of beliefs involves the perceived trustworthiness of other nations. It is reasonable to presume that the U.S. public will be most likely to support programs that involve nations that are viewed as reliable allies. Recent poll data identifies some potential problems.[6] The list of nations that are seen as trustworthy allies presents no surprises, such as Canada, Federal Germany, Japan, and Mexico. Potential difficulties are evident, however, given the set of nations that are not perceived as being trustworthy, which includes states that have been central in recent U.S. security programs, for example, the Republic of Korea, Turkey, and Jordan.

A final significant pattern concerns public support for defense spending.[7] In recent years military aid programs (as opposed to straightforward commercial sales) have been reestablished in new forms through the use of payment deferrals, below-market interest rates, and forgiveness of debts. From an economic standpoint, these actions are equivalent to aid grants.

Hence the relevance of trends in public support for the increased levels of defense spending needed to fund these and other programs. By 1980 support for increased defense spending had reached levels not seen since the Korean War era. These preferences persisted until late 1981, when a modal preference for maintenance of then current levels of spending began to dominate. By March 1982, 41 percent of the public believed that increases in military expenditures had been excessive, and a plurality of the public preferred cuts in defense spending as a means for reducing the federal deficit, as opposed to cuts in other areas or increases in taxes.

Recent Public Assessments of Economic and Military Assistance

The most recent data regarding the U.S. public's assessment of economic and security aid programs is provided by a 1982 Gallup poll sponsored by the Chicago Council on Foreign Relations.[8] Since this is one of a series of polls sponsored by the Chicago Council, trends in the public's evaluation of assistance programs can be seen. Furthermore, since the Council sponsored two surveys—a sample of the general public and a poll of leaders—the views of these two segments of the public can be compared.

Public assessments of economic aid programs are of concern for several reasons (see tables 4–2 and 4–3):

Most obviously, economic assistance is often consciously employed to achieve national security objectives, for instance, the rationales presented for the Caribbean Basin Initiative.

From some standpoints, economic and military aid are inter-

Table 4–2
Attitudes Regarding U.S. Economic Assistance, 1982

Overall Attitude toward Economic Aid
The question: On the whole, do you favor or oppose our giving *economic* aid to other nations for purposes of economic development and technical assistance?

Attitude toward Economic Aid	*1974* %	*1978* %	*1982* %	*Change in Points 1978–1982*
Total Sample				
Favor	52	46	50	+4
Oppose	38	41	39	−2
Not Sure	10	13	11	−2
Total	100	100	100	
Elite Sample				
Favor		90	94	+4
Oppose		7	4	−3
Not Sure		3	2	−1
Total		100	100	

Source: Adapted from John E. Reilly (ed.), *American Public Opinion and U.S. Foreign Policy, 1983* (Chicago: Chicago Council on Foreign Relations, 1983), p. 25.

Table 4–3
Effect of U.S. Economic Aid to Other Countries

The question: Do you feel economic aid to other countries generally:

Total Sample					*Elite Sample*			
	1974[a] %	*1978*[a] %	*1982* %	*Change in Points 1978–1982*		*1978* %	*1982* %	*Change in Points 1978–1982*
Helps Our National Security					*Helps Our National Security*			
Yes	44	45	44	−1	Yes	71	78	+7
No	45	44	43	−1	No	25	17	−8
Not Sure	11	11	13	+2	Not Sure	4	5	+1
Total	100	100	100		Total	100	100	
Helps the National Security of Other Countries					*Helps the National Security of the Other Countries*			
Yes	65	72	68	−4	Yes	81	83	+2
No	24	16	20	+4	No	15	10	−5
Not Sure	11	12	12	0	Not Sure	4	7	+3
Total	100	100	100		Total	100	100	
Helps Our Economy at Home					*Helps Our Economy at Home*			
Yes	25	34	30	−4	Yes	62	69	+7
No	65	54	57	+3	No	33	22	−11
Not Sure	10	12	13	+1	Not Sure	5	9	+4
Total	100	100	100		Total	100	100	
Gets Us Too Involved in Other Countries' Affairs					*Gets Us Too Involved in Other Countries' Affairs*			
Yes	73	75	75	0	Yes	34	27	−7
No	17	16	17	+1	No	62	63	+1
Not Sure	10	9	8	−1	Not Sure	4	10	+6
Total	100	100	100		Total	100	100	

Source: Adapted from J.E. Reilly (ed.), *American Public Opinion and U.S. Foreign Policy, 1983* (Chicago: Chicago Council on Foreign Relations, 1983), p. 25.

[a]The 1974 and 1978 questions read: "Do you feel that giving U.S. economic aid to other countries generally:"

changable. A nation can be provided with a million dollars in security assistance. Alternatively, a nation can be given a million dollars in development aid and allowed to reprogram the same amount of money from other accounts into its military budget.

Some segments of the public (as shown below) perceive a connection between U.S. economic aid and subsequent U.S. military involvement.

Several interesting patterns are present in these responses. A substantial—78 percent—and growing majority of the leadership sample believes that these economic assistance programs contribute to U.S. national security interests. The general public, in contrast, splits evenly on this question. Very large majorities in both groups believe that economic aid contributes to the national security of recipient nations.

A division with considerable political import occurs regarding the effect that economic aid programs have on the traditional U.S. foreign policy goal of containing communism. A plurality of the public believes that these programs do not have this effect, while a majority of the leadership sample disagrees.

A comparable division occurs regarding the prospect that economic aid will lead to excessive levels of U.S. involvement in foreign nations' affairs, with a large majority of leaders not perceiving this as likely, while an even larger majority of the public sees this as a danger. The public's negative assessment of this facet of the economic aid program has not changed significantly since 1974.

From the standpoint of an administration or Congress attempting to use economic aid as an instrument of the national security policy, these are not encouraging results. Major differences exist between the leaders surveyed and the public at large. The patterns present little cause for optimism concerning public support for major economic aid initiatives (for example, the early 1984 Kissinger Commission proposals), because the public at large regards such initiatives as the precursors of military involvement.

Turning to military assistance, there is solid (63 percent) opposition among the general public to concessionary forms of military aid, up 5 percent since 1978, and a majority (53 percent) opposed to military sales (see tables 4–4 and 4–5). The only consolation is the increase since 1978 in the percentage of the public favoring sales, which grew by 6 percent to 39 percent. In short, the public would prefer that the United States sell military equipment rather than give it away, but would prefer that it do neither. As was the case previ-

Table 4–4
Attitudes Regarding Security Assistance, 1982

Overall Attitude toward Military Aid

The question: On the whole do you favor or oppose our *giving* military aid to other nations? By military aid I mean arms and equipment, but not troops.

On the whole do you favor or oppose our government *selling* military equipment to other nations?

	Total Sample					*Elite Sample*		
Attitude toward Giving Military Aid	*1974* %	*1978* %	*1982* %	*Change in Points 1978–1982*	*Attitude toward Giving Military Aid*	*1978* %	*1982* %	*Change in Points 1978–1982*
Favor	22	29	28	−1	Favor	60	59	−1
Oppose	65	58	63	+5	Oppose	33	31	−2
Don't Know	13	13	9	−4	Don't Know	7	10	+3
Total	100	100	100		Total	100	100	
Attitude toward Selling Military Aid					*Attitude toward Selling Military Aid*			
Favor	35	33	39	+6	Favor	67	68	+1
Oppose	53	54	53	−1	Oppose	26	24	−2
Don't Know	12	13	8	−5	Don't Know	7	8	+1
Total	100	100	100		Total	100	100	

Source: J.E. Reilly, (ed.) *American Public Opinion and U.S. Foreign Policy 1983* (Chicago: Chicago Council on Foreign Relations, 1983).

Table 4–5
Effect of U.S. Military Aid to Other Countries

The Question: Do you think that giving military aid to other countries generally:

	Total Sample				*Elite Sample*		
	1974 %	*1978* %	*1982* %	*Change in Points 1978–1982*	*1978* %	*1982* %	*Change in Points 1978–1982*
Helps Our Own National Security							
Yes	36	35	37	+2	66	65	−1
No	51	50	48	−2	29	25	−4
Not Sure	13	15	15	0	5	10	+5
Total	100	100	100		100	100	
Helps the National Security of Other Countries							
Yes	69	72	71	−1	87	76	−11
No	21	16	16	0	10	13	+3
Not Sure	10	12	13	+1	3	11	+8
Total	100	100	100		100	100	
Helps Our Economy at Home							
Yes	31	43	39	−4	75	69	−6
No	58	44	49	+5	22	25	+3
Not Sure	11	13	12	−1	3	6	+3
Total	100	100	100		100	100	
Helps the Economy of Other Countries							
Yes	60	59	55	−4	40	31	−9
No	27	25	29	+4	52	58	+6
Not Sure	13	16	16	0	8	11	+3
Total	100	100	100		100	100	

Table 4–5 continued

The Question: Do you think that giving military aid to other countries generally:

	Total Sample				*Elite Sample*		
	1974 %	*1978* %	*1982* %	*Change in Points 1978–1982*	*1978* %	*1982* %	*Change in Points 1978–1982*
Aggravates Relations with Other Countries							
No	67	73	na		65	na	
Yes	18	14	na		26	na	
Not Sure	15	13	na		9	na	
Total	100	100			100		
Strengthens Our Political Friends Abroad							
No	43	46	na		72	na	
Yes	40	39	na		20	na	
Not Sure	17	15	na		8	na	
Total	100	100			100		
Is a Good Substitute for the Use of American Troops and Manpower							
Yes	44	49	51	+2	70	68	−2
No	34	33	31	−2	21	19	−2
Not Sure	22	18	18	0	9	13	+4
Total	100	100	100		100	100	

Helps Prevent the Spread of Communism							
Yes	36	34	35	+1	53	54	+1
No	48	48	47	+1	39	33	−6
Not Sure	16	18	18	0	8	13	+5
Total	100	100	100		100	100	
Gets Us Too Involved Other Countries' Affairs							
Yes	78	79	78	−1	55	53	−2
No	13	12	14	+2	41	38	−3
Not Sure	9	9	8	−1	4	9	+5
Total	100	100	100		100	100	
Lets Dictatorships Use Their Military Power against Their Own People							
Yes	59	61	65	+4	73	68	−5
No	16	16	14	−2	18	19	+1
Not Sure	25	23	21	−2	9	13	+4
Total	100	100	100		100	100	

ously, the leadership sample results stand in contrast, with sizable majorities favoring both grants and sales. The decline in the percentage of "don't know" responses among the public is also of interest—positions may be hardening.

Other points of interest include the following:

While a majority of the leadership sample believes that military aid promotes U.S. security interests, a plurality (48 percent–37 percent) of the general public disputes this proposition.

Both samples agree that security assistance promotes the national security interests of the recipient nations. The percentage of the leadership adhering to this view, while still substantial (76 percent), has diminished by 11 percent since 1978, however, with a concomitant increase in those undecided.

Leaders perceive that the United States receives economic benefits from military aid; a plurality of the public disputes this proposition and the percentage of skeptics has increased by 5 percent since 1978.

In an interesting reversal, a majority of the public believes that security assistance assists recipient nations' economies, although the percentage has dropped by 4 percent since 1978. In contrast, only 31 percent of the leadership sample accepts this proposition, 9 percent fewer than in 1978.

In 1978, large majorities in both samples believed that security aid tended to aggravate U.S. relations with other nations. A smaller plurality among the public at large and a firm majority of leaders further held that such aid strengthened our political friends abroad. (Results from 1982 are not available for this item or the next.)

A majority of the general public and a significant majority of leaders hold that security assistance is a good substitute for the use of U.S. troops. A significant percentage of the general public is undecided on this issue (18 percent).

Containment as a rationale for U.S. security aid programs is not persuasive to a plurality of the general sample (47 percent to 35 percent) but is accepted by 54 percent of the leadership sample.

A sizable majority of the general sample (78 percent) and a majority of leaders (53 percent) agree with the proposition that security assistance promotes excessive levels of U.S. involvement in the affairs of other nations.

Significant (roughly two-thirds) majorities in both samples believe that military aid reinforces the power of dictatorships vis-à-vis their own populaces.

Projections, even to the immediate future, are difficult given the short time periods in which these trends change. If the most recent patterns and trends continue, however, the implications for the military assistance program are clear. There are some optimistic findings, such as the belief of majorities in both samples that security assistance is a good substitute for U.S. forces.

The overall patterns for the public at large are, however, negative from the vantage points of administrations and members of Congress who support current programs. The containment rationale for security assistance is rejected by a plurality of the public at large. A plurality of the public also believes that the program does not serve U.S. national security interests. A majority of the public opposes both concessionary aid and military sales.

Interest Groups

A wide range of special-interest organizations attempt to influence security assistance policy. To understand the roles that these groups play in the development of military assistance programs, three questions need to be answered:

Which groups attempt to influence the program, and for what reasons?

How can these groups have an impact on security assistance policy? What resources and mechanisms can they employ?

How have groups attempted to use these resources to influence recent security assistance decisions?

Interest Group Motivations to Influence Security Assistance Policy

Interest groups perform several functions in the legislative process. One role is to count the house. Since legislative outcomes often involve coalition-building and compromise, interest groups need to contact members of Congress, including members who may not be likely to support their positions, to determine the balance between supporters and opponents (one needs to have a head count before deciding how much compromise is in order), and to identify both the intensity of opposition and the reasons for disagreement.

The last point is of particular importance. By identifying the frameworks within which members approach issues, groups can develop more effective ways of presenting their positions. For example, a member might be very concerned with Soviet presence in a region, while attaching little importance to regional balances not involving the Soviets. As discussed below, the most productive appeals are likely to be those that are congruent with members' definitions of the problems at issue.

Interest groups also contact likely supporters in the Congress and administration. They do this to alert members to the significance of proposed legislation, to reinforce support, and to encourage members to take leading roles on legislation. Again, identification of the frameworks members use to define the problems at issue is important, because success is likely to be associated with the development of a proposed policy that aligns with members' mental maps of the problems and associated solutions.

A second class of functions involves information. For more than a decade Congress has played a more active role in the formulation of all aspects of national security policy. Concomitant with this increased activism has been an expansion of its involvement in other spheres of policy, for example, the new budget process. This overall increase in activity places a premium on the use of lobbyists as (for want of a better term) "extended staffs." In this function, interest groups assist members by providing information, assisting in the development of approaches and compromises, counting support in the houses, and developing legislative strategy.

Electoral activity is a final set of functions. An interest group has its greatest potential impact in nonlobbying activities (defining lobbying for the moment to encompass what groups do in Washington). The best scenario for any interest group is to appeal to members who are already in substantial agreement with its position. To be sure, even supporters will differ concerning details (for example, what mix of assistance instruments should be employed?). From the standpoint of an interest group, however, these are much easier questions to address, given basic agreement on the problem and candidate solutions. Many groups place a premium on district-level electoral activities, ranging from contributions to get-out-the-vote campaigns.

Similar considerations help to explain the continuities that have characterized the security assistance program, notably the tendency for a few nations to receive most of the funds and to recur in this favored position throughout the history of the program.

Given the prominence of Israel in the program, it is common to rate AIPAC, the most prominent lobby working on its behalf, as the superstar of lobbying. Without attempting to disparage its accomplishments (AIPAC strikes us as a well run, effective organization), we suggest that this is an incomplete explanation to the extent that it focuses on lobbying, narrowly defined. If AIPAC is the principal reason for Israel's position, how did Turkey, which has no comparable champion, get near the top of the list?

The answer we propose is foreshadowed in the preceding argument. Since 1947, Israel has figured both prominently and favorably in the world views of both the public at large and members of government.[9] Given its high standing in these cognitive maps, plus the fact that many of the other most favorably regarded nations have not, since postwar recovery, required-security assistance (for example, the United Kingdom), Israel's position comes as no surprise. To be sure, disagreements exist regarding the amounts and form of aid to be provided. Nevertheless, we suggest that even if AIPAC were to be incompetent (which it is not), Israel would still have stood near the head of the queue.

Groups Concerned with the Entire Program. Security assistance policy does not have a highly visible impact on most congressional districts and states. Although of considerable economic importance for a few regions, such as the areas in which export fighter aircraft are produced, it has little obvious district-level impact elsewhere.

This lack of visibility may contribute to the program's relatively low standing in public opinion. It also may be behind one of the most striking characteristics of the program—the fact that few groups express an interest in the entire (world-wide) security assistance program, as opposed to projects targeted at specific regions.

In recent congressional deliberations, only one organization has regularly come forward as an advocate for the entire program—the American League for Exports and Security Assistance, Inc. (ALESA). As the name suggests, ALESA is a trade promotion coalition. Its member organizations are corporations and trade unions which benefit from U.S. military aid and sales programs.[10] In recent presentations in congressional hearings, ALESA has supported administration arguments in favor of the program. In terms of the belief systems identified in the earlier review of opinion leaders' views, these arguments are most congruent with the cold war internationalist frame of reference.

As an advocate, ALESA operates with two disadvantages. The first is that its corporate members' interests are sometimes divergent, for example, ALESA represents competing corporations that produce fighter aircraft for export. When this occurs, these firms have an obvious incentive to focus their lobbying efforts on behalf of their own products, instead of working through the all-industry structure that ALESA provides.

The small number of trade union members is a second disadvantage. Particularly noteworthy is the absence of the International Association of Machinists, the largest of the aerospace unions. Furthermore, even among member unions security asistance may not be a high priority compared to other legislative goals.

Relatively few groups oppose the security assistance program in its entirety. In recent years, opposing testimony representing this opposition has usually come from coalitions of religious organizations (for example, the Interreligious Task Force on U.S. Food Policy), with the argument being that resources should be devoted instead to economic and humanitarian aid. In terms of the modal tendencies found for opinion leaders in the preceding analysis, this position is most congruent with the belief system of post-Cold War internationalism, as opposed to the Cold War internationalist norms cited by ALESA in its presentations.

Strikingly absent from the statements of both opponents and proponents of current levels of security assistance spending is the subject of negotiated restraints on the transfer of arms to Third World nations. This topic was the subject of the U.S.–Soviet Conventional Arms Transfer (CAT) talks as recently as December 197
collapse of the CAT negotiations, this topic appears to hav
from the nation's political agenda.[11]

Groups Concerned with Portions of the Program. Organiz
attempt to influence security assistance policy generall
very specific interests. For corporations, these include n
are potential customers, given the right credit and aid
other organizations, particular nations and regions are
This focusing of organization's participation has three cor
for members of the executive and legislative branches.

The first follows from the narrow range of interests, wh
it more difficult to coordinate and reach agreement concerning the overall program. A group that is successful in its lobbying may have more money allocated to its favored nation at the expense of other recipients, even though it is indifferent (rather than opposed) to U.S. programs directed at these other states.

A second consequence follows from the relatively unique standing of security assistance among the policy instruments that the

United States government employs in its foreign policy. Much of the foreign policy process is conducted completely within the executive branch. Congress can exercise oversight over these processes, but often only after the fact.

In the case of security assistance, however, yearly congressional appropriations are required *before* the executive branch can take action. Hence, members have more opportunities to affect policies prior to their implementation, and groups can also have influence prior to implementation if they can convince members of Congress to support their positions.

As a consequence, interest groups attempt to influence security assistance policy for two reasons. Most obviously, a group might be concerned with a specific facet of the program (for example, AIPAC's concern with the strength of Israel's armed forces). In addition, however, security assistance is viewed and valued as a lever that can be used to influence a broad range of foreign policy actions—in effect, it serves as a proxy for a wider range of policies. This increases the complexity of security assistance deliberations. Groups that have no significant interest in the program may attempt to influence it to affect other facets of foreign policy.

A third consequence follows from the ways in which interest groups approach the specific segments of the program that are of concern to them. There are strong points of continuity between the representations made by organizations and the divergent patterns of opinion identified in elite views which make it more difficult to develop agreement.

Examples are provided in the recent testimony of Thomas A. Dines, Executive Director of the American Israel Public Affairs Committee (AIPAC) and David J. Sadd, Executive Director of the National Association of Arab Americans (NAAA), on the topic of security assistance in the Middle East. It comes as no surprise that their positions differ. The form that their disagreement takes, however, has considerable significance for the program.[12]

References to the Soviet Union's involvement in the Middle East, a point of concern to the Reagan administration, serve as an illustration. In Dines's statement considerable emphasis is placed on Israel's strategic importance to the United States, an importance which is construed, in large part, in terms of the Soviet Union's actual and potential involvement in the region. Sadd's presentation, in contrast, is striking because of its lack of references to Soviet presence in the area. Indeed, the absence of military considerations or assessments of regional balances in the NAAA presentation is noteworthy.

Continuing with the example, another pattern of interest occurs. AIPAC testimony contains themes which relate to all three of the elite world views identified previously, with some emphasis being given to the Cold War frame of reference, using Soviet activities in the theater as a rationale for aid to Israel. NAAA testimony, in contrast, eschews the Cold War frame of reference, presenting a world view that is more in consonance with the post-Cold War internationalism.

The important point is not that the two spokespersons disagree (one would hardly expect otherwise). What is significant, rather, is how they disagree.

It would have been possible for both sides to have agreed on all or at least most of the facts at issue, for example, that Soviet presence in the theater was at a given level. Even more importantly, it would have been possible for the two sides to have used a common frame of reference to give meaning to these facts—within the framework of Cold War beliefs, for instance, specified levels of Soviet military presence would be a subject of concern for the United States. Given these points of continuity, the two sides could then have argued details such as the ratio of aid for Israel to assistance for bordering nations.

Such continuities do not occur in the presentations cited. To a large extent, Sadd and Dines work within different frames of reference, and cite different "facts." It is not simply that they disagree but that they are dealing with different (self-defined) problems. Their depictions of the problems to be addressed and recommended courses of action have little in common.

In security assistance, as in any area of policy, decision-making in both branches of government is facilitated to the extent that consensus exists among interested parties concerning the facts of concern, policy objectives, and the means that are appropriate for achieving those objectives. To the extent that such consensus is lacking—as is evident when interest groups differ to the degree seen here—it becomes much more difficult to formulate a consensus policy that will be consistent over time.

The Impact of Interest Groups on Security Assistance Policy

Interest groups can have an impact on security aid policy only by acting through members of the executive and legislative branches.

Assessments of attempts to influence policy often focus on lobbying, defined narrowly to encompass the formal and informal presentations which organizations make to members of government. Lobbying, in turn, is often discussed in terms that would be appropriate for the description of a formal college debate—the presentation of a position, which is compared with that of the person being lobbied, and point–counterpoint debate. Recent research indicates that this is, at best, an incomplete representation of the ways in which groups lobby and otherwise attempt to influence policy.

It is certainly true that interest groups contact members of Congress to make persuasive appeals. Other (possibly more basic) objectives and processes also enter into play, however. Key considerations in this regard are the concepts of the "scripts" which policy makers may employ and these same leaders' "cognitive maps."

Even in a single day, organizations and individuals encounter a wide range of problems and situations. Observing their behavior, regular patterns tend to be evident. Similar problems are met with comparable types of responses. The notion of scripts has been developed by artifical intelligence researchers to account for the orderliness and predictability of human behavior.[13]

The core of the argument is that people (acting individually or in organizations) would be overwhelmed if they attempted to deal with each situation they encountered as a unique event. Instead, it appears that people reduce complexity by grouping what are defined as similar situations into sets, each of which is associated with a script that defines appropriate and inappropriate types of actions.

The concept of scripts is important because of the way in which it links descriptions (of the problems being addressed) and prescriptions (ranges of appropriate "solutions"). Working within this framework (and assuming the existence of one or more scripts), it is apparent that the definition of a policy problem becomes the critical factor in government deliberations because these definitions have associated with them ranges of appropriate policy actions.

The concept also has the interesting corollary that organizations and individuals should have a great deal of difficulty dealing with what are perceived as new situations for which no existing script is appropriate—a phenomenon not unknown in government deliberations.

The notion of a script can be linked to the idea of a cognitive map. These maps are world views or strategic perspectives that outline the elements of a problem as perceived and potential courses of action, precisely the elements that enter into a script.[14] Research on policymakers' cognitive maps has indicated that leaders' perceptions of policy problems are extremely complex, indicating the value of scripts as mechanisms for making problems more manageable. Research has also shown that deliberation within policymaking bodies often does not assume the form of point–counterpoint argument concerning alternative courses of action. Available evidence suggests instead that policy debate may be a two-step process. In the first step, efforts are made to construct a common map of the problem(s) being addressed, without which parties are (literally) not debating the same problem. Incremental adjustment of positions and point–counterpoint debate follows, and to a large extent, presupposes, the creation of this common reference map.[15]

The three modal tendencies found for American leaders' views (Cold War internationalism, post-Cold War internationalism, and nationalism) can be viewed as constituent elements of scripts and cognitive maps. For example, a given level of Soviet military presence in the Middle East might be a very prominent feature in the cognitive map of a person who operates within the Cold War frame of reference. Such presence might be associated with a range of recommended counteractions. For a post-Cold War internationalist working with a different script and map, the same level of presence may not be a prominent terrain reference and may not have the same associated (scripted) response.

Previous analysis has shown that senators debating security assistance to Greece and Turkey acted in manners which were consistent with the argument that their positions were based on their cognitive maps of the points at issue, and that these maps had moderate to strong resemblances to the three modal tendencies identified for elite public opinion (post-Cold War internationalism, et cetera).[16]

Given the vantagepoints of scripts and cognitive maps, a different perspective on interest group lobbying emerges.

How Have Interest Groups Attempted to Influence Policy?

Given the preceding arguments concerning the importance of scripts and cognitive maps, we have some expectations as we turn to examine recent attempts by interest groups to influence security assistance policy. The core point to be addressed is the extent to which groups attempt to influence policy by presenting a definition of the problem that entails group-favored solutions.

To the extent that the preceding arguments are correct, we anticipate that interest groups' presentations to Congress will present cognitive maps that are consonant with those presented in on-the-record remarks by at leat some of the members who are in general agreement with the groups' positions.

Concerning the maps themselves, the employment of a relatively large number and range of themes or concerns can be anticipated, which provide an overall strategic context in which security assistance problems and solutions are located. Given the absence of large amounts of district-level impact, narrowly focused arguments should not be likely.

Little overlap should be found between the maps of the problem constructed by opposing interest groups, because each should, given the preceding arguments, be attempting to sell a world-view and a set of policy recommendations associated with that strategic view that is significantly different than that presented by groups with opposing interests.

Finally, given the patterns found in U.S. leaders' views, the three modal frameworks of Cold War internationalism, post-Cold War internationalism, and nationalism can be expected to be found in different groups' (and different legislators') depictions of the problems to be addressed.

The 1978 Senate debate concerning the Carter administration proposal to lift the embargo on security assistance to Turkey provides a useful test case.[17] In 1975 Turkish forces conducted two invasions of Cyprus. Following the second incursion, an embargo was established on further U.S. security assistance to Turkey. In response, Turkey placed restrictions on U.S. facilities in Turkey, to include intelligence-related installations. Although some exceptions were allowed in the intervening years, an embargo was still in force in 1978, when the Carter administration proposed its elimination.

The evidence to be reviewed comes from congressional deliberations and hearings concerning the embargo. To provide a baseline for the evaluation of interest groups' presentations, a content analysis of the remarks of eight senators (four proponents of the embargo and four supporters of the administration position) who assumed leading roles in the floor debate on this issue was completed. This analysis identified nineteen themes that were used by the members to define their positions. These themes provide a sketch outline of the cognitive maps and scripts that these members used to address the perceived points at issue.[18] This same set of themes was used as a benchmark for the evaluation of the positions advocated by interest groups in their testimony to Congress concerning the embargo, again on the assumption that the sets of themes employed (and, equally important, not employed) outline the maps and scripts employed by the groups. (Table 4–6 outlines the positions taken both by the set

Table 4–6
Views of Interest Group Spokesmen and Senators Concerning the Turkish Arms Embargo

Summary of Themes[a]	*Interest Group Spokespersons*			
	Pro[b]		*Con*	
	Ali	*Rush*	*Alexandrides*	*Rossides*
1. The key legal point—sanctions following a violation of U.S. law—has been made by imposition of the embargo to date; there is no need for further punishment.				
2. [Opposite of 1.] Turkey has not been sufficiently punished; the embargo should be maintained in support of the principle of law.	(−)		X	X
3. Because of the embargo Turkey's military strength has deteriorated.	X	X		
4. [Opposite of 3.] The embargo has not been enforced, hence no deterioration.				
5. NATO has been affected negatively by the embargo.	X	X		
6. [Variant of 5.] Point accepted; importance for U.S. discounted.			X	X
7. Loss of access to Turkish facilities has degraded U.S. intelligence collection capabilities.	X			
8. [Variant of 7.] Point accepted; importance for U.S. discounted.			X	X
9. Greece's security interests will be affected positively by lifting the embargo.	X	X		

[a]Numbers index themes cited by speakers. Instances in which speakers mentioned themes for the purpose of arguing that they were not important facets of the situation are indexed by "(−)", that is, Mr. Bakar Ali's dismissal of the legal precedents theme.

[b]Pro-proponent of Carter administration proposal to lift Turkish arms embargo.

Selected Senators							
Pro				*Con*			
Byrd	*Bentsen*	*Chafee*	*Bartlett*	*Biden*	*Percy*	*Kennedy*	*Sarbanes*
X	X	X					
				X	X	X	X
X	X	X	X				
				X	X		
X	X	X	X				
				X	X		
X	X	X	X				
				X			
X	X	X	X				

Table 4–6 continued

Summary of Themes[b]	Interest Group Spokespersons			
	Pro[a]		Con	
	Ali	Rush	Alexandrides	Rossides
10. [Opposite of 9.] Negative impact on Greek security interests if embargo were lifted.			X	X
11. Dangerous precedent—Saudi Arabia or other recipients of U.S. arms may be less likely to honor U.S. restrictions on use of weapons if the embargo is lifted.	(−)			X
12. Violations of human rights on Cyprus by Turkish forces.	(−)		X	X
13. The Turkish Government is deliberately threatening or blackmailing the U.S.			X	X
14. [Opposite of 13.] Turkey is not making such threats as a deliberate government policy; negative consequences may be likely, but due to public opinion or other factors not under the control of the Turkish Government.	X	X		
15. Continuation of the embargo promotes a just settlement on Cyprus.				
16. [Opposite of 15.] Continuation does not promote a settlement.	X	X		
17. New Turkish regime is more flexible, more interested in settlement; favorable outcome more likely.				

[a]Numbers index themes cited by speakers. Instances in which speakers mentioned themes for the purpose of arguing that they were not important facets of the situation are indexed by "(−)", that is, Mr. Bakar Ali's dismissal of the legal precedents theme.

[b]Pro-proponent of Carter administration proposal to lift Turkish arms embargo.

Selected Senators							
Pro				*Con*			
Byrd	*Bensten*	*Chafee*	*Bartlett*	*Biden*	*Percy*	*Kennedy*	*Sarbanes*
				X			
					X		X
						X	X
				X	X		
X	X	X	X				
				X	X	X	X
X	X	X					
X	X						

Table 4–6 continued

Summary of Themes[a]	*Interest Group Spokespersons*			
	Pro[b]		*Con*	
	Ali	*Rush*	*Alexandrides*	*Rossides*
18. Recent proposals by Turkish Cypriots make a just settlement more likely.	X			
19. [Opposite of 18.] Proposals do not make a just settlement more likely; need to wait and see.			X	X

[a]Numbers index themes cited by speakers. Instances in which speakers mentioned themes for the purpose of arguing that they were not important facets of the situation are indexed by "(−)", that is, Mr. Bakar Ali's dismissal of the legal precedents theme.

[b]Pro-proponent of Carter administration proposal to lift Turkish arms embargo.

of senators whose views are used as reference points, and the interest groups.)

With the senators, whose expressed views serve as the benchmarks for this assessment, patterns consistent with the expectations are evident. The members whose views are presented placed the issue in a variety of contexts that created an overall map within which this particular question was to be addressed.

Furthermore, there is no overlap between the maps of the problem and associated courses of action traced by proponents and those traced by opponents. To the extent that this involves the themes presented as paired opposites, this comes as no surprise. The same pattern would occur in a formal debate.

Of even greater significance, however, are the instances in which a lack of overlap occurs because members on the opposite side of this issue do not include a particular factor in their field of reference. For example, charges of human rights violations by Turkish forces on Cyprus and the potential precedents that might be created for other recipients of U.S. arms are cited by opponents of the administration position, but not by supporters. By the same token, some supporters of the administration position make reference to changes in Turkey's government that do not enter into the assessments of proponents.

Similarly, all four supporters of the administration position cite the importance of U.S. intelligence collection facilities in Turkey; only one opponent, Senator Joseph R. Biden, Jr., referenced these installations, and then by referring to them as convenient, but hardly

Selected Senators							
Pro				*Con*			
Byrd	*Bensten*	*Chafee*	*Bartlett*	*Biden*	*Percy*	*Kennedy*	*Sarbanes*
X	X						
				X		X	

essential. There is little resemblance between these facilities cited by Senator Biden and the installations valued by the four supporters of the administration position.

These and other differences (traced in table 4–6) show the merit of the map and script metaphors. In the 1978 deliberations members were not debating a single issue or even an agreed-upon set of concerns. Instead, they were presenting and defending divergent world views of considerable sophistication and complexity that had a number of points which were not in common. In a literal sense, they were discussing different issues, and these differences in the description of the problem entailed different policy recommendations.

Turning to the four interest groups representatives' statements, patterns consonant with our expectations are once again evident. Each speaker presents a complex depiction of the situation at issue. These outline maps link the specific question at issue with a wide range of other concerns, including such issues as the strength of the NATO alliance (for proponents of the administration position) and human rights policies (a major policy theme during the Carter administration that was emphasized by opponents).

As previously, there is little overlap between proponents and opponents. When overlaps occur (for example, Mr. Hasan Bakar Ali's remarks concerning potential precedents for other recipients of U.S. arms in theme 11), the point is raised to make the argument that it should not be regarded as an important factor. While specific points, such as the importance of the U.S. intelligence installations in Turkey, were debated, the more general profile is a divergence in world views, rather than a more narrowly focused debate. Once again, qualitatively different problems were defined, with divergent policy recommendations being associated with these definitions.

Furthermore, general congruences are evident between the maps of the problem traced by the interest groups and those members of the Senate who took positions favored by the groups. For example, both members and interest groups speaking in favor of the administration position expressed concern with what they saw as the weakening of the NATO alliance's position by the embargo and with the importance of full access to the intelligence facilities located in Turkey. Similarly, both congressional and interest group opponents tended to emphasize human rights concerns. This is precisely the profile to be expected, given the cognitive maps and scripts arguments—the presentation by interest groups of relatively complex definitions or descriptions of the problem at issue that align with members' world views.

By the same token, reflections of the divergent vantage points identified in the assessment of U.S. leaders' views are also apparent. For example, proponents of the administration position in 1978 placed emphasis on themes relating to competition with the Soviet Union—the need to strengthen the Turkish armed forces and thereby enhance NATO's position vis-à-vis the Soviets and the importance of the intelligence facilities. These themes are constituent elements of the Cold War belief system. Opponents, on the other hand, tended to emphasize other factors, including human rights concerns and what were perceived as the legal principles at issue, which are more congruent with the post-Cold War internationalist belief system.

This is not to suggest that any of the speakers whose views have been examined were rigid ideologues—the sophistication of their assessments belies such an interpretation. Nor is it to imply that NATO is of no consequence to those working largely within the post-Cold War framework or that those who emphasized the (perceived) East–West dimensions of the issues in 1978 were unconcerned with human rights.[19]

The point, rather, is a more general one. Since Vietnam, there has not been consensus among U.S. opinion leaders concerning the standards by which foreign policy should be assessed. At least three divergent belief systems have been identified. In this analysis we see reflections of these divergences in the assessment of security assistance issues. In recent security assistance deliberations, participants have been dealing with different (self-defined) problems for which different mixes of policy solutions are appropriate. To the extent that these divergences persist, the development of consensus support for the program becomes more difficult.

Assessments and Recommendations

Summary

This study has examined two important constituencies for security assistance programs—the general public and interest groups—in a period characterized by more active congressional involvement in the formulation of these programs.

A review of recent poll data revealed little support for the program among the general public. From the standpoint of the government officials attempting to use security assistance as a policy instrument, results were somewhat more encouraging when the views of leadership groups were examined.

In reviewing the views of these leaders, however, significant divergences were identified which have a potential bearing on military aid and sales programs. Since Vietnam, consensus no longer exists concerning the standards by which U.S. foreign policy should be evaluated. Instead, three distinct groups have been identified.

The first is a group which continues to accept the pre-Vietnam and pre-Watergate Cold War norms that have been used as a rationale for security assistance programs by all administrations since Truman's. This group is the most natural audience for the security assistance program.

The second group are post-Cold War internationalists. This group believes in the continuation of active U.S. participation in international affairs, but with emphasis on a different, less militarily oriented, mix of policy instruments.

The final group consists of post-Cold War nationalists, whose belief system gives priority to domestic problems, posits a scaling-down of U.S. involvement in world affairs, and regards U.S. military involvement abroad, including military assistance programs, with considerable skepticism.

Among interest groups, it was found that few groups are concerned with the security assistance program as a whole. When groups express an interest in the program, it is often not because of their concern with military assistance but rather because the program offers one of the most accessible ways of influencing other facets of foreign policy.

Analysis of interest groups' attempts to influence the security assistance program placed emphasis on the cognitive maps and scripts which are employed to define policy problems and which entail divergent courses of action. Examination of recent security assistance deliberations suggests that both government officials and interest groups construct such maps and scripts. From this vantage point, attempts at persuasion are efforts by groups to promote world views that are consonant with those of government officials; debate and argumentation in their narrow classical forms play lesser roles. These divergent world views reflect the differing strategic perspectives found among leadership groups. The net result is to make the development of consensus support for the security assistance program more difficult.

Recommendations

By presenting recommendations, our objective is to improve consensus support for the security assistance program absent which consistent (and hence effective) policy is not possible. Security assistance should not be the only foreign policy instrument employed, but it should be available.

More active congressional involvement in the formulation and implementation of the program will continue. This increased participation provides more opportunities for constituencies, acting through members of Congress, to affect the program. Furthermore, Congress' more active involvement is an advantage to the extent that increased executive and legislative branch consensus can be fostered. Foreign audiences are also likely to take note of such consensus.

The basic problem to be addressed is a divergence in strategic perspective or world-views. Without consensus, how can a coherent and consistent policy be developed?

Our first recommendation is that proposals to decouple consideration of economic and military assistance programs be opposed. Given observed cleavages among leadership groups, this is precisely the wrong thing to do. Among the two internationally oriented groups identified, those who accept the Cold War containment paradigm are likely to be more supportive of military programs, while post-Cold War internationalists are more likely to support economic aid. Separation of military and economic aid is likely to be a formula for failure. Indeed, attempts should be made to more closely link the two, both to maximize the appeal of the consolidated package and to assist in the integration of the two programs.

Second, Congress needs to be provided with more and better leverage points. At present, the initial stages of program development are largely conducted within the executive branch. The security assistance program is presented to Congress only after it has been put into what is intended as final form.

Two changes are needed. The first is to solicit and respond to contributions from members of Congress and their staffs in the program preparation phase. A good rule of thumb in legislative process is that formal hearings should be boring because most of the potential points of controversy have already been resolved. This would entail more legislative liaison interactions on the part of Department of Defense and Department of State personnel; more contacts with interest group representatives; and a more decentralized and continuous approach to the development of program proposals, including interactions with members who do not sit on committees with direct oversight responsibilities for the program.

In addition, Congress needs to be provided with more and better leverage points. Security assistance programs presently are required to serve as proxies for a host of foreign policy initiatives that are less subject to congressional control. One candidate mechanism consists of the policy guidance documents promulgated at the secretarial level within the administration. DOD components are required to justify their proposed actions within these frames of reference.

There is merit in extending the distribution of these documents, particularly when they are in draft form. Given that the Congress is ultimately going to make decisions that affect the implementation of these proposals, it makes sense to have its contributions early in the process. This would not provide this or any other administration with everything it wants. It would, however, allow congressional responses to be more narrowly focused on issues for which the security assistance program is presently forced to serve as a proxy. Given responsiveness on the part of the executive branch, a likely outcome would be a security assistance program that is not necessarily an administration's ideal choice, but which has greater consistency—and therefore force—over time, a tradeoff that we see as acceptable.

Congress also should be provided with better access to intelligence information, and the legislative branch's intelligence analysis capabilities should be increased, possibly by increasing the Congressional Research Service's role in this area and by providing it with greater access to executive branch data. The increase in Congress's involvement in the formulation and reconciliation of the budget created a requirement for the Congressional Budget Office. By the same token, Congress's increased participation in the formulation of security assistance and other facets of foreign policy creates a requirement for improved procedures to ensure that members receive the information they need in order to be informed participants.

This will help to alleviate a problem seen in the 1978 Turkish arms embargo debate where proponents of the executive branch's position relied on administration presentations for support while opponents employed less qualified public statements made years previously by Ford administration spokesmen that did not reflect the most recent developments. In other policy arenas, interest groups can serve members of Congress by providing estimates comparable in quality to those produced by the administration, such as economic forecasts. For the most part, however, outside groups cannot perform this function during security assistance deliberations.

This change would go considerably beyond current intelligence committee oversight procedures. At the same time, however, the success of these committees in protecting sensitive information suggests that it is feasible.

Once again, this change would not result in an administration obtaining support for all of its proposals. It would, however, enhance the quality of deliberations. This is consistent with our advocacy of more and earlier congressional involvement in the development of security assistance programs.

Notes

1. John E. Reilly, *American Public Opinion and U.S. Foreign Policy in 1979,* (Chicago: Chicago Council on Foreign Relations, 1979), p. 4.

2. B.L. Page and R.Y. Shapiro, "Effects of Public Opinion on Policy," *American Political Science Review* March 1983, pp. 175–190; R.B. Mahoney, Jr., "The Superpower Balance, Military Policy, and Public Opinion in the United Kingdom, France, and the Federal Republic of Germany," in D. Daniel (ed.), *International Perceptions of the Superpower Military Balance,* (New York: Praeger, 1978.)

3. O.R. Holsti and J.N. Rosenau, "Cold War Axioms in the Post-Vietnam Era" in O.R. Holsti et al. (eds.) *Change in the International System* (Boulder: Westview Press, 1980), pp. 263–301; "Does Where You Stand Depend on When You Were Born? The Impact of Generation on Post-Vietnam Foreign Policy Beliefs," *Public Opinion Quarterly* 44 (Spring 1980), pp. 1–22; "America's Foreign Policy Agenda: the Post-Vietnam Beliefs of American Leaders" in C.W. Kegley and P.J. McGowan (eds.) *Challenges to America: United States Foreign Policy in the 1980s,* (Beverly Hills: Sage, 1979); and "Vietnam, Consensus, and the Belief Systems of American Leaders," *World Politics* 32, (October 1979), pp. 1–56.

4. Reilly, *American Public Opinion.*

5. For example, the October 1981 *Newsday* poll results reported in A. Richman, "American Attitudes Toward Building and Exercising Military Power Since Vietnam." Paper presented at the annual meeting of the International Studies Association, 1982, Table 1.

6. Yankelovich/Time poll, December 1981, presented in Richman, "American Attitudes," table 7.

7. Polls assembled by Richman, "American Attitudes," tables 9 & 10.

8. Reilly, *American Public Opinion and U.S. Foreign Policy.* (Chicago: Chicago Council on Foreign Relations, 1983).

9. For example, the poll data summarized in Richard H. Curtiss, *A Changing Image: American Perceptions of the Arab–Israel Dispute,* (Washington, D.C.: The American Educational Trust, 1982).

10. The membership of the American League for Exports and Security Assistance (ALESA):

Companies

Aerojet General Corp.
American Hoist and Derrick Co.
AM General Corp.
AVCO Corp.
Beech Aircraft
The Boeing Co.
Control Data Corp.
Dusommon Inc.
Elexco International
Emertson Electric Co.
Fairchild Industries
FMC Corp.
Garrett Corp.
Gates Learjet Corp.
General Dynamics Corp.
Goodyear Aerospace
Harsco Corp.
Hazeltine Corp.
Hughes Aircraft Co.
Hughes Helicopters
Lear Siegler, Inc.
Lockheed Corp.
McDonnell Douglas Corp.
Martin Marietta Aerospace
The Mead Corp.
NAPCO Industries
Northrop Corp.
Pneumo Corp.
Raytheon Company
Rockwell International
Rohr Industries
The Singer Corp.
Sundstrand Corp.
Teledyne, Inc.
TRW, Inc.
United Technologies Corp.
Vought Corp.
Westinghouse Electric Corp.

Unions

Communications Workers of America, AFL-CIO
International Brotherhood of Teamsters, Chauffeurs, Warehousemen, and Helpers
Marine Engineers' Beneficial Association, AFL-CIO
United Brotherhood of Carpenter's and Joiners of America, ALF-CIO

11. A good review of this topic is provided in Andrew J. Pierre, *The Global Politics of Arms Sales* (Princeton: Princeton University Press, 1982).

12. Statement by Thomas A. Dines, Executive Director, American Israel Public Affairs Committee (AIPAC), Subcommittee on the Near East and South Asia, Senate Committee on Foreign Relations, March 2, 1983; written

testimony of David J. Sadd, Executive Director of the National Association of Arab Americans, same committee and date.

13. Roger C. Schank and Robert P. Abelson, *Scripts, Plans, Goals and Understanding,* (Hillsdale, N.J.: Lawrence Eribaum Associates, 1977).

14. Robert Axelrod (ed.), *Structure of Decision,* (Princeton: Princeton University Press, 1976).

15. I. William Zartman and Maureen R. Berman, *The Practical Negotiator,* (New Haven: Yale University Press, 1982).

16. This analysis is presented in chapter 4 and appendices A and B of Ernest Graves (ed.), *U.S. Security Assistance in the 1980's,* unpublished manuscript, study for the Defense Security Assistance Agency (DSAA), (Washington, DC: Georgetown University CSIS, 1983).

17. Additional information concerning the 1978 decision and other recent security assistance deliberations is provided in Graves, *U.S. Security Assistance.*

18. This analysis is presented in greater detail in Graves, *U.S. Security Assistance.* The Senators' remarks analyzed were taken from the principal floor debate on the issue, as presented in the *Congressional Record,* July 25, 1978. Interest group statements are taken from *International Security Assistance Programs, Hearing before the Subcommittee on Foreign Relations,* Senate, 95th Congress, 2d session, April 25–May 2, 1978; *Foreign Assistance Legislation for Fiscal Year 1979, hearings and markup before the Committee on International Relations,* House, 95th Congress, 2d session, April 5–May 3, 1978; *The Military Aspects of Banning Arms Aid to Turkey, hearings before the Committee on Armed Services,* Senate, 95th Congress, 2d session, June 28, 1978. The themes presented employed a crude, but useful, summaries of speakers' remarks. These themes facilitate the comparison of statements and the identification of overall patterns; they do not provide an exhaustive summary of speakers' positions.

19. Furthermore, we suspect that individuals (inside or outside of government) may employ more than one of these frameworks. For example, a member (or group) may use the norms of Cold War containment to evaluate policy problems involving NATO's Central Front while relying on a post-Cold War internationalist perspective in assessments of issues involving the Third World. The key point, as we see it, is the employment of scripts, even if different scripts/frames of reference are employed for different (self-defined) classes of situations.

5
Implications for the Future of Security Assistance as an Instrument of Defense and Foreign Policy

Ernest Graves

Introduction

What lessons learned from the first four chapters help most in understanding the paradoxical attitude in Americans toward security assistance, and how can such understanding help in reaching decisions about the program? The aim of this chapter is to pull the threads together, offer a composite view of the role of the program as a policy instrument, and suggest ways to deal with all the controversy that surrounds and infuses the decision process.

Nothing in the CSIS study[1] dispelled the impression held before that security assistance had been, is today, and is likely to be for the foreseeable future a major instrument of U.S. foreign policy. Even the severest critics recognized this point while decrying that it should be so.

It appeared at the outset, and the study confirmed, that the security assistance program is highly political. Groups with competing objectives are constantly trying to influence government policy. In politics perception is often more important than substance. One could even say that perceptions are the substance—"the reality"—of politics. Viewed in this light, the challenge in government decision making is to relate perception and substance so as serve the public interest.

One of the most striking lessons from the preceding chapters is the extent to which perceptions of security assistance vary. Not only the evidence presented, but also the views of the authors reflect quite different perceptions of the state of the program and its contribution to U.S. foreign policy and national security. All the authors agree, however, that over time such differences have grown rather than diminished.

There have always been critics of foreign aid. It has never been a program with a broad domestic constituency. However, the divergence of views today is far more serious than the differences expressed when, following World War II, the focus of our aid was rebuilding the economies and the military strength of our wartime allies. These differences have had a significant impact on both program decisions and the contribution of the program to security. Whether this is good or bad is also subject to debate. Some see such differences as undermining our world posture. Others see them as helping us to reach the most advantageous course.

One aim of the CSIS study was to assess the potential for reaching a greater measure of consensus that would enhance the program's contribution as an instrument of foreign policy and national defense. Such consensus would not necessarily mean a greater use of security assistance. The program would benefit from a greater measure of agreement on when it should and should not be used.

To address policy implications, it is helpful to focus on perceptions of three major aspects of security assistance:

the rationale for the program;

the cost; and

the decision process.

Analysis of these aspects leads naturally into a discussion of implications for the future of the program and what might be done about it.

Overview of Findings

A historical review of the security assistance program reveals a strong relationship between the U.S. employment of security assistance and the major international developments of the last thirty-five years. This is the major point developed by Grimmett in chapter 1. The other point of historical significance is the number of examples of both success and failure where security assistance was a major instrument of policy.

Since the end of the last world war there have been two pillars of U.S. strategy: nuclear deterrence and collective security. Nuclear deterrence has worked; we have avoided general war.

We have asked much more of collective security, and the record has been mixed. There has been a whole series of lesser conflicts. We have sought to deter open hostilities, to limit them, and to settle all manner of conflicts by a system of collaboration among like-minded countries. We have employed security assistance as the principal means to secure and to bind all these collective security arrangements. We have used it as a quid pro quo for overseas bases and transit rights, for the settlement of disputes between friends, and generally to secure the cooperation of allied and friendly states across the spectrum of military and political affairs. Security assistance has been an almost universal tool of foreign and defense policy.

Overall, collective security, supported by security assistance, has been a success and has made a decisive contribution to peace and stability in important regions of the world. However, it has not guaranteed successful protection of U.S. interests. We know this particularly from the experience of Vietnam, but also from the series of conflicts between India and Pakistan and from the fate of countries such as Ethiopia and Iran. The result has been serious debate and sharp disagreement as to whether security assistance should continue to be the "universal" instrument of policy that it has in the past.

The public record and media reporting of the annual security assistance program deliberations from 1959 through 1982 are rich sources of information about perceptions of the program. In chapter 2 Hildreth identified and traced themes in executive branch testimony, committee reports and floor debates that reflect the main views of the times. For example, there is remarkable constancy in the anti-Communist justification of the executive branch. The reactions of Congress to the program have followed recurring themes, as well, but there has been a trend from general support to greater skepticism about the purposes and the effectiveness of security assistance. Media reporting and commentary have changed the most, with early supporters like the *New York Times* and the *Washington Post* now asking the most questions and early critics like the *Chicago Tribune* and the *Wall Street Journal* now much more supportive.

From the extensive series of discussions with individuals and in groups that were the basis for chapter 3, Kramer gives the reader a good understanding of the approach of the executive branch and the Congress in reaching decisions about the program. For example, these discussions highlighted the significance of the OMB "mark" and congressional budget targets in determining the overall size of the program, the different weights attached to the military, diplomatic, and political justifications by the departments and the congressional committees, and the highly political nature of many of the decisions.

There has been some excellent research done on the role of public opinion and interest groups in decisions on the foreign assistance program, but much remains to be learned. Mahoney highlights in chapter 4 the low level of support for security assistance among the general public, the favorable attitude of the majority of the opinion leaders, the narrow focus of most interest groups and the complex way in which these different factors ultimately influence the decisions of the leaders in the executive branch and the Congress.

These points have a major bearing on perceptions of the rationale, the cost and the decision process for the security assistance program.

The Rationale

As already noted, the executive branch rationale has remained essentially the same since the program's inception. The United States has world-wide interests that are vital to its security and economic well-being. These interests are threatened by Soviet expansionism and regional conflict. Cooperation with allied and friendly governments in a system of collective security is the best way to confront these threats. Security assistance provides the added resources and the symbolic ties to make collective security work. Collective security, supported by security assistance, provides the protective shield behind which political, economic, and social development can progress. Such progress provides the basis for independence and international stability.

While the rationale has remained constant, the world environment has changed significantly. The locus of the active military confrontation between the United States and its allies on the one hand and the Soviet Union and its allies on the other has shifted from Europe and Northwest Asia to the Third World—the Near East and Southwest Asia, Southeast Asia, Africa, and Latin America. The Soviet Union has achieved at least strategic nuclear parity with the United States. We have evolved from a situation in which nuclear deterrence and collective security were highly complementary to one in which, for much of the world, we must rely almost entirely on collective security to deter aggression and cope with hostilities if deterrence fails. It is part of the paradox that in spite of this shift there seems to be less support for relying on security assistance as a policy tool.

Congress and the public no longer accept the traditional rationale as they once did. Overseas interests are acknowledged but with widely varying perceptions of their importance. There is even less unanimity as to the extent to which these interests are truly threatened. Perceptions of the threat tend to depend upon perceptions of relative importance.

Experience has led to skepticism about the reliability of allied and friendly governments and hence about the efficacy of collective security. The contribution of security assistance to collective security is viewed as more symbolic than substantial. Members of Congress—and to a significant extent top political appointees in the executive branch—view security assistance primarily as a tool for acquiring political influence, rather than as a means for improving military capabilities to cope with a genuine threat.

Just as many in the Third World have difficulty understanding why the Soviet Union and the United States give such priority to building up and modernizing nuclear armaments directed at each other, so many in the United States fail to comprehend the seriousness of the regional threats that lead our Third World partners to devote so much attention to arming themselves against their neighbors.

Security assistance is not perceived as either guaranteeing cooperation when the purposes of the recipient and the United States diverge or necessarily affording the recipient the means to cope with the most serious threats to its own security.

Needless to state, these varied perceptions have a significant impact on the decision process and the program that results.

The Cost

The cost of security assistance is viewed in both relative and absolute terms. It involves not simply money, but also the risk of commitment to the security of another country, the effect on the United States, our image and our self-esteem if the recipient somehow falls short, and the even greater impact if the entire enterprise fails, as most perceive it did in cases such as Vietnam and Iran.

The executive branch views the cost as very modest compared to the importance of the objectives sought and the ends achieved. Comparisons with economic indicators and the levels of other programs support this view as far as the monetary cost is concerned. In terms of purchasing power for the equipment, training, and support that it provides, on-budget military aid in 1983 was only 5 percent of what it was at its peak in the early 1950s. The entire security assistance program, including guaranteed FMS credits and ESF, was only 28 percent of the 1952 level in constant dollars.[2] For FY 1983 the security assistance program was 0.2 percent of the GNP, 1 percent of federal outlays, and 4 percent of national defense outlays. In 1952 it was 2 percent of GNP, 8 percent of federal outlays, and 13 percent of national defense outlays.[3] These figures do not necessarily demonstrate that the program today is not large enough—only that it is not large in historical perspective.

Congressional and public views of the cost are more often relative than absolute. They tend to be influenced by the person's view of the U.S. interest, the threat and the character and reliability of the assisted government. When these are all viewed positively, the main concern is "how much is needed." When these aspects are not viewed favorably, the cost is criticized—as too high, a "give-away" or worse. It may be human, but it is certainly American, to find all kinds of fault with the way money is spent if one does not see clearly how one benefits from the expenditures.

A question frequently asked members of the executive branch and the Congress is why there is so much difficulty in obtaining the level of funds that the president requests. When the conversation is frank, almost invariably the response is that it is not the amount of money, which is not great, but rather disagreement over the policy of military support for the government of the country involved.

Sometimes this disagreement is laid out specifically in committee reports or limitations in actual law. More often it is expressed indirectly by requirements for greater funding of other countries without an overall increase, leaving reduced amounts for the less favored countries.

On the average since 1950 Congress has passed a security assistance program that was 12 percent below the president's request. For FY 1976 through FY 1982 the final program averaged 3 percent smaller than the administration's budget.[4] In relation to this experience the 14 percent reduction resulting from the continuing resolution for FY 1983 appears relatively severe, particularly with the impact of earmarking. Still, foreign more than fiscal policy appears to be the issue that really causes such cuts.

One aspect of cost is increasingly the focus of attention—the debt owed the United States from the FMS financing program and the effect of further loans on the economies of the recipients. Since the inception of the present credit program in FY 1969 the United

States has loaned foreign governments more than $25 billion for the purchase of U.S. military equipment and support. At the beginning of FY 1983 the principal amount of loans outstanding was $15.6 billion.[5]

Several perceptions about this program deserve mention. It was widely believed that improving world economic conditions justifed a switch from grants to loans. It was also theorized that such a switch would help restrain arms transfers. The huge debts of some of the main recipients of FMS loans and the growth of world-wide arms sales, particularly sales to U.S. credit recipients, seem to contradict these earlier perceptions.

Now there is concern that some of our most important debtors may not be able to repay the loans and that their defaults will have serious repercussions for the entire foreign assistance program. For most countries the FMS debts are a small fraction of their total debts and can be handled as part of a general rescheduling. However, interim shortfalls have to be met from the FMS guarantee reserve fund, and the necessity to replenish this fund has a highly visible impact on the security assistance budget. At the same time there is growing sentiment that the United States should not aggravate the situation by extending additional FMS credits at high interest rates to countries with serious debt problems. Rather, grants or highly concessional loans should be provided. The provision of on-budget concessional loans and the increase in MAP grants and forgiven loans proposed by the administration for FY 1985 are much needed responses to the economic straights of the recipients of most U.S. military assistance.

As far as risks are concerned, the executive branch generally views the risks from inaction as outweighing the risks of involvement. However, the view of the general public and many in Congress is quite different. Whether or not they can accept the monetary cost, the risk of U.S. involvement in armed hostilities represents a potential cost that they are generally not willing to incur.

The Decision Process

The decision process is extremely complicated, involving as it does many departments and agencies of the executive branch, at least six congressional committees and the 535 members of Congress, numerous interest groups, and a large public with diverse views. The mechanics of the process involve many technicalities and nuances. However, what makes the process really complicated is its highly political nature and the interplay of a multitude of views, based on quite different perceptions of the purpose and utility of security assistance.

The executive branch views Soviet expansionism as ubiquitous and seeks to counter it by effective management of relations with all countries seen as prepared to resist Soviet influence, interference or intervention. There are, however, shifts in priority as events unfold, relations with other governments change, or our perceptions of them vary.

Crises, such as the outbreak of conflict, internal upheaval, the need to arrest a deteriorating situation, or an opportunity to negotiate peace, have a greater effect on the security assistance program than the year-to-year effort to shore up resistance to Communist expansion. Crises capture everyone's attention and provide the political basis for decision.

A change in the U.S. administration can produce a pronounced shift in the way the executive branch views a foreign government, particularly a dictatorship.

In sum, the executive branch views security assistance as a prime tool of the strategy of collective security and of foreign relations.

Several factors appear to influence Congress and its deliberations on the security assistance program. Certainly the members feel a deep sense of responsibility for the security of the United States. This inclines them to support security proposals from the chief executive and commander-in-chief. On the other hand, members are naturally highly sensitive to the views of their constituents—the general public—and jealous of their prerogatives as a separate and coequal branch of government.

The fact that the majority of the general public does not support security assistance cannot fail to influence congressional attitudes toward the program. When they can speak frankly, members of Congress explain that they have to get reelected, that foreign assistance is not a popular subject with their constituents, and that they do not have the time to educate them. While not all subscribed to this view, almost all expressed the belief that the president can be more persuasive on this subject than anyone else—that he must exercise his leadership and speak out to convince the electorate of the need for our involvement abroad and our foreign assistance programs.

Congress views foreign aid deliberations as the means to exercise influence, if not control, over the conduct of foreign policy. Members have their own foreign policy views. For many the lesson of Vietnam is to guard against commitments that could lead to direct engagement of U.S. forces in armed conflict when our strategic interest is only marginal. A majority in Congress has always supported the basic concept of security assistance—the indispensible tool for implementing collective security arrangements against Communist expansionism and regional instability. At the same time Congress reflects the natural American skepticism about both the ends and the efficacy of foreign assistance. Concern about human rights is not only a matter of natural repugnance at supporting a regime whose conduct we abhore. As a practical matter, most people in the United States view dictatorships as inherently unstable. All this leads us to expect—even demand—that recipients of our aid give evidence of respecting our standards for relations between the government and the people. The result is the ultimate foreign policy dilemma: How much are we prepared to become involved with the other countries of the world in order to preserve and enhance our interests abroad?

The political heat generated by the contention between the executive and the Congress over some security assistance measures belies the claim that domestic issues completely overshadow foreign policy in the minds of the electorate and their representatives in Congress.

The leadership group strongly favors foreign assistance, but the majority of the public accords it low priority. The 1982 poll of the Chicago Council on Foreign Relations reported 59 percent of the "leaders" in favor of military aid, but only 28 percent of the "general public."[6]

The Vietnam War caused a major swing in the public attitude toward security assistance. Before the war the public accepted the rationale that security assistance was a way to prepare our allies and friends to handle local and even regional conflicts without the need for direct U.S. involvement. After Vietnam security assistance came to be perceived as entangling the United States with countries that would not always be able to cope with threats to their security, with the risk that U.S. forces might well be required to honor our commitments, expressed or implied.

The CSIS review of the record of executive and congressional deliberations, of media reporting and commentary, and of the interviews with policymakers confirmed findings of other scholars that there are distinctly different views of the world.[7] These different perspectives of world affairs lead to quite different conclusions about the degree of danger to U.S. national interests and the best means to promote our national well-being.

One group holds to views that were more widely held during the Cold War—abiding concern over soviet expansionism and the belief that to secure our interests we must counter the Soviets with a combination of our own military power and assistance to allied and friendly states to the maximum extent that resources will allow.

Another group—sometimes known as the "post-Cold War internationalists"—also has concern over expansionist moves by the Soviet Union, but believes that the United States can best secure its international interests by employing a variety of policy instruments with less military emphasis.

A third group—the "post-Cold War nationalists"—gives priority to domestic problems, believing that the key to preserving U.S. well-being is maintaining our economic strength and improving our social fabric so that we will have the means and the cohesion to resist any serious foreign encroachment.

According to mood theory, the U.S. attitude toward relations with the rest of the world undergoes broad swings of twenty to thirty years' duration.[8] The present period could be characterized as an "introvertive" or relatively "isolationist" phase, the last major shift in mood having come during the Vietnam War. If this theory is correct, it may be another decade before the pendulum swings back to more of a consensus that security assistance is an effective deterrent and one of the best ways to strengthen defense cooperation and enable allied and friendly states to provide for their own security.

Interest groups see the decision process in both the executive branch and the Congress as an opportunity to wield influence in favor of clients or constituencies. Often their objectives are quite narrow. Some, however, are broadly supportive of security assistance or broadly opposed. To the extent that the preferences of a number of interest groups are reflected in a particular authorization or appropriation bill, their combined support is definitely a factor when it comes to a committee or floor vote on the measure.

Implications for the Future

Just as the 1950s and 1960s were overshadowed by the experience of World War II and Korea, so the 1970s and 1980s are overshadowed by the experience of Vietnam. Different groups view this experience differently.

The executive branch tends to believe that we had good reasons for resisting the takeover of the South by North Vietnam, but that our approach was seriously flawed and the American people would not continue to support what clearly became a losing cause.

The Congress and the public tend to believe that the United States cannot hope to control or influence events everywhere in the world, that we lack both the resources and reliable partners, that the risks are too great, and that we must establish priorities and focus our effort on the problem areas of greatest importance.

Beyond this difference in view over the extent to which the United States should try to manage the world is an equally important difference over the extent to which resistence to communism requires resort to force. Because the Communists espouse violence as a normal policy instrument, the rhetoric of anticommunism tends to emphasize the exercise of power and the capability to employ force.

However, the political leaders and the people of the Western democracies are not generally comfortable with the prospect of having ultimately to engage in hostilities to preserve their way of life against Communist expansion; they prefer to believe that there are other, essentially peaceful ways.

Security assistance was once viewed as such a way, leading to sharing the burden of preparedness and, through preparedness, deterring conflict. Vietnam changed this perception, probably for at least a generation.

The future of the security assistance program depends on world developments and the skill of efforts made to concert the actions of the executive branch and the Congress. As far as world developments are concerned, if the American people feel genuinely threatened, they will be willing, even impatient, to resort to force. We have not seen much evidence of this feeling since the early years of the Vietnam conflict. However, the studies of historical swings in the U.S. mood indicate a high probability that it will return, particularly in the face of clear danger. On the other hand, if the threat is in an area of the world not generally considered important and is below the threshold of blatant aggression, the American people will not be aroused, and they will not see the need to risk a forceful response.

As far as concerted action is concerned, the Constitution provides for the separation of powers, and the executive and the Congress have been contending with each other since the beginning of the Republic as to their respective responsibilities in the area of foreign policy. There is not room here to chronicle all the swings of this pendulum. Suffice it to say that in today's world foreign assistance authorizations and appropriations represent the practical way that the Congress has to influence the day-to-day, week-to-week, and month-to-month conduct of foreign policy. While the executive may bridle at such constraint of its freedom of action, for the most part foreign policy appears better served by accommodation than by confrontation. The psychological impact of security assistance on both friendly governments and potential enemies is bound to be weakened if the U.S. government is perceived as divided in its support of the aid recipient.

Each branch of government is understandably jealous of its powers and prerogatives. The situation is aggravated when the administration and one or both houses are of different political parties. Political campaigns engender opposing views, and elected officials feel compelled to act on their campaign rhetoric. However, such post-election swings tend to be dampened after a year or so, and the course of foreign relations trends back toward a middle road. The ground lost in such swings is not easily recovered.

Partisanship in foreign affairs can be viewed in two ways. On the one hand, partisan debate can produce cathartic and creative results in the foreign policy and defense establishments. On the other hand, it can be highly disruptive and adversely affect relations with both friendly and hostile states. How to reconcile the need for innovation with the need for coherence and continuity is a perennial problem in government.

Conclusions

Several conclusions flow from this review and analysis.

First, we should not count on reconciling the divergent views of security assistance in the 1980s. Diverse views of the world and the role of the United States on the world scene are now too firmly rooted in U.S. predilections and experience. The shift in mood discussed earlier is not going to happen overnight. Theory and analysis suggest that it will occur with time. Only a serious crisis would galvanize public opinion in the near term. Our country is better off with the present difference of views than we would be with the extreme international danger needed to bring about an early bipartisan consensus on the subject of military aid.

Second, the difference of views and lack of public support do not mean that the administration and the Congress are powerless to act in the national interest. Political leaders differ on this point, but a significant number believe that, in the area of foreign policy and assistance programs, the leadership can do what they believe is best for the country without the specific support of the electorate and without fear that their stand will have a significant effect on the outcome in future elections. This is not to say that forthright action will not have political repercussions—only that the leadership can stand the impact if they will.

Third, the security assistance program has not fared badly in terms of gross funding levels. Nor is there really serious opposition to military assistance per se. The disagreements concern policy questions about our relations with particular countries whose governments are in trouble whether from external threats, internal policies, or adverse economic and social conditions beyond anyone's power to correct in the short term—or, most often, a combination of all three. Military aid to such countries gets "squeezed" when Congress accords them lower priority within overall budget constraints.

Fourth, there is an ebb and flow of relations between the executive branch and the Congress—between confrontation and collaboration—that has a serious effect on the conduct of foreign affairs. The convening of the Scowcroft Commission on Strategic Forces, the Carlucci Commission on Security and Economic Assistance, and the Kissinger Commission on Central America all reflect a recognition of the need for greater collaboration in the face of serious threats to the United States. The Reagan administration could not have gained the participation of important members of varied persuasion in these endeavors without such recognition. While bipartisan commissions may not be the panacea for all that troubles relations between the executive and the Congress, they are one example of what can be done to communicate better and to develop practical working relations that lead to sound solutions in the national interest notwithstanding significant differences in world views.

Efforts should not be confined to additions to the law or formal arrangements. On the contrary, success may depend upon informality and a spirit of cooperation. As one member of Congress said recently, "The Administration should not be up here on the Hill negotiating with the committees under the lights. There ought to be a way to work out a mutually acceptable program in advance and win sufficient bipartisan support to pass it without the confrontation that seems to happen every year."

The recent Supreme Court decision nullifying the legislative veto makes it all the more important to seek greater accommodation between the executive and the Congress. Some in Congress would use the decision as a pretext for further circumscribing executive authority to sell arms without specific congressional review. However, the decision can be viewed as an opportunity to maintain the initiative in relations between the two branches. To the extent that the president continues current practices as a matter of comity, without conceding any legal point, he retains the lead and forestalls congressional moves to circumscribe executive flexibility. He could go further and seek through private and informal contacts to involve members of Congress earlier in the formulation of the security assistance program. Unless the administration is aggressive in providing for congressional participation, the backlash against the Supreme Court decision is likely to result in even more restrictive laws. If they are vetoed and the veto is sustained, relations will be even more acrimonious, the program will suffer, and so will relations with allied and friendly governments.

Fifth, the president must take the lead in "educating" the people of the United States about foreign policy and the importance of foreign assistance. Members of Congress have made clear their belief that congressional races are seldom, if ever, decided by issues of foreign relations but that foreign assistance is not a popular subject with the majority of their constituents. They would like to leave the main burden of public discussion to the president. At the same time they have expressed the need for greater public acceptance if members of Congress are to provide more support for the security assistance program.

In the second half of his term, with his domestic agenda well along and several critical foreign policy issues demanding his attention, President Reagan began speaking out on international issues. Of course, with the unfolding of the 1984 presidential campaign, there was the quadrennial risk that the discussion of foreign affairs would degenerate into petty competition for partisan advantage.

The sixth conclusion concerns planning. As a problem in planning, the security assistance program is a miniature version of our own defense program spread among 100 countries. However, there is a great contrast between the elaborate planning, programming, and budgeting and the extensive consultation with Congress that support the formulation of the U.S. defense program and the limited consultation and planning that go into the formulation of the security assistance program. This is not to suggest a return to the practice—long since abandoned as ineffective and wasteful—of trying to make the development of the security assistance program a fully integrated part of the DOD planning, programming, and budgeting process. It is also well to note the significant improvement in planning since the low point early in the Carter administration. Then it was virtually abandoned under the policy that arms transfers were to be used only as an "exceptional tool."

It must be recognized that the impact of international developments and political factors in the later stages of program deliberations often limit the utility of security assistance planning. Nevertheless, if the executive branch is to bring the Congress into the process at an earlier stage, the reach of planning should be extended, outyear program amounts should be more than plug numbers to help in projecting total budgets, and recipient countries should know better what, and what not, to expect. The last should help in managing the continual negotiation for "most-favored-nation" treatment that characterizes many of our security assistance relationships.

There is a seventh and final point concerning process. The political leadership should never take for granted or flag in its support of sound management of the security assistance program. There is too little recognition of the effort involved in and the contribution to our foreign relations from the effective day-to-day management of security assistance. This is a vital element in the spectrum of relations between the United States and allied and friendly governments—from the top political leaders down to the members of a U.S. mobile training team instructing allied officers and men in the use and care of equipment supplied through our security assistance program.

Having praised the contribution that such activity makes, one must sound a note of caution. Much as our assistance is valued, we should not develop exaggerated ideas about the amount of influence it affords us. As noted earlier, there is a widespread view that we can and should expect recipients of our aid to improve their behavior according to our standards. It was reasoned that this was not simply a matter of favoring our own ways. Americans believe that long-term stability depends upon the consent of the governed and that this can be assured over time only by a proper regard for the people's welfare. Nevertheless, it is generally unrealistic to expect diverse peoples around the world immediately to adopt our ways in return for no more than our friendship and the quite limited support that we are able to provide in the early stages of most security assistance programs.

It is too bad that many people's perception of security assistance management comes only from an endless series of critical GAO reports. The deficiences derive mostly from the sheer size and complexity of the program, but they have to be corrected. The program needs the confidence of the public, of our own political leadership and of the recipient countries. However, there is an even more important management task: to scrub continually the national decision-making apparatus—both within the executive branch and between the executive branch and the Congress—to counteract the tendency to build up bureaucratic impediments to agreement and action. This is not to suggest any radical reorganization or change in personnel. Either of these steps would do more to disrupt the program than to enhance it. The entire decision-making process needs well-trained, experienced, and highly motivated career professionals—responsive to policy direction, but able to provide continuity in program formulation and execution.

If one looks at the turbulence in this program over the last six years—in policy, in personnel, and in priorities—and then one looks at what has been accomplished in spite of it, one has to believe that security assistance is capable of making an important contribution to U.S. objectives in the 1980's.

The foregoing conclusions have concerned primarily process rather than policy. With the diversity of views encountered, there is no ready basis for suggesting any broad shift in policy that would be likely to attact greater support for the program. There are, however, two points to make about policy.

First, there is often an unfortunate separation between security and economic assistance in policy statements, in program presentations, and in the development of policy and programs at the Washington level. Efforts at integration have been only partially successful. This results in a perception that we lack a coherent policy. The complementarity of the various assistance programs is more evident at the level of the U.S. missions to the recipient countries. Without necessarily launching some radical reorganization, the executive can make further progress in integrating the various types of foreign assistance and making a unified presentation of the policy and the program to the Congress.

Second, the executive needs to win congressional approval of a much more realistic policy on the financing of equipment, training, and support for our less-developed collective security partners. The size of the security assistance program compared to the overall federal budget is sufficiently small that we should not have to resort to off-budget credits to finance 70 percent of our military assistance program. The current depletion of the FMS loan guarantee reserve fund is just the tip of the iceberg of problems that we can look for in the future if we do not put the program on a sound financial footing. This is the sort of problem where consultation with Congress should in time produce a practical long-term solution.

The CSIS study of security assistance began in the midst of the 1982 congressional campaign and gained momentum during the lame duck session of Congress that disposed of the president's FY 1983 security assistance budget request with a continuing resolution. In the following months it was intriguing to see, in both the executive branch and the Congress, principals and staff members coming to many of the same conclusions reached in the study. Whether this will lead to a better outcome for the program remains to be seen. However, the ongoing effort to improve communications, explain the program, and achieve more effective consultation is a real improvement and augurs well for the future of security assistance and the contribution it will make to the collective security of the free world.

Notes

1. The results of the CSIS study are incorporated in a final report entitled, U.S. Security Assistance in the 1980's, Center for Strategic and International Studies, Georgetown University, July 1983.

2. Based on data from Congressional Presentation Document, FY 1984 (CPD) and the DOD inflation index compiled by Len Campbell.

3. Based on data from Federal Government Finances, 1984 Budget Data, Office of Management and Budget, February 1983.

4. Based on data from the CPD.

5. Ibid.

6. Reilly, John E., *American Public Opinion and U.S. Foreign Policy 1983*, (Chicago: Chicago Council on Foreign Relations, 1983), p. 25.

7. The world views discussed here coincide with the group views identified by O.R. Holsti and J.N. Rosenau in "Cold War Axioms in the Post-Vietnam Era," in *Change in the International System*, (Boulder: Westview Press, 1980).

8. See the works of Frank L. Klingberg starting with "The Historical Alternation of Moods in American Foreign Policy," *World Politics*, January 1952; Steven A. Hildreth, "The American Public and the Future of U.S. Foreign and Defense Policy," in Robert Kupperman and William J. Taylor, Jr. (eds) *Strategic Requirements for the Army to the Year 2000* (Lexington, Mass.: Lexington Books, 1984), pp. 23–49 and William B. Taylor, Jr., *The Future of Conflict, The Washington Papers* (Boulder, Colo.: CSIS and Praeger, 1983).

Appendixes

Appendix A

Important Benchmarks in Legislative History of Security Assistance Program

Year	*Legislative Enactment*	*Result*
1947	Greek–Turkish Aid Bill (P.L. 80-75)	First major commitment of military and economic aid
1948	Marshall Plan (Economic Cooperation Act of 1948) (P.L. 80-472)	Major commitment of economic aid to rebuild Europe
1949	Mutual Defense Act of 1949 (MDAA) (P.L. 81-329)	Creates Military Assistance Program (MAP); creates authority for Foreign Military Cash Sales
1951	Mutual Security Act of 1951 (P.L. 82-165)	Establishes authority for military and economic assistance in one legislative vehicle; establishes basis for Economic Support Fund (ESF) concept
1954	Mutual Security Act of 1954 (P.L. 83-665)	Establishes basis for Foreign Military Credit Sales
1961	Foreign Assistance Act of 1961 (P.L. 87-195)	Makes major consolidation of all prior Security Assistance Programs in new legislative vehicle
1968	Foreign Military Sales Act of 1968 (P.L. 90-629)	Establishes separate legislative authority for Foreign Military Cash and Credit Sales Program
1976	International Security Assistance and Arms Export Control Act of 1976 (P.L. 94-329)	Creates Arms Export Control Act which consolidates existing legislation relating to U.S. arms sales (cash or credit), government and commercial; establishes International Military and Education as separate program from MAP; Mandates phase-out of MAP
1978	International Security Assistance Act of 1978 (P.L. 95-384)	Establishes Economic Support Fund (ESF) as title for program previously known as Security Supporting Assistance, Supporting Assistance and Defense Support
1981	International Security and Development Cooperation Act of 1981 (P.L. 97-113)	Provides authority for a Special Defense Acquisition Fund (SDAF) to facilitate procurement of high demand items in anticipation of foreign military sales to eligible nations

Appendix B

Selected Major International Events, 1946–1981, Having Major Implications for U.S. Policy Interests

Years	*Events*
1946–1947	Major economic problems throughout Europe; consolidation of Soviet control over Eastern European governments; Greek Civil War; Soviet pressures on Turkey and Iran
1948	Communist coup in Czechoslovakia; Berlin blockade begins
1949	Communist victory in Chinese Civil War; Soviet Union explodes atomic device
1950	North Korea invades South Korea; Korean War begins lasts until 1953
1954	French forces defeated in Indochina; Vietnam partitioned
1954–1955	Quemoy and Matsu crisis in Formosa strait
1956	Suez crisis; Soviets crush Hungarian uprising
1958	King of Iraq assassinated; Lebanon crisis leads to intervention of U.S. marines
1959	Fidel Castro seizes power in Cuba
1962	Cuban missile crisis
1963–1965	Conflict in Vietnam escalates
1967	Six Day War in Middle East between Israel and Arab states
1968	Tet offensive in Vietnam; Czechoslovakia invaded by Soviet and Warsaw Pact military forces
1973	October War between Israel and Arab states; Vietnam peace agreement
1978–1979	Iranian revolution, Shah overthrown; Khomeini assumes power
1979	Israeli–Egyptian peace treaty signed; Soviet military invasion of Afghanistan
1980	Iran–Iraq war begins
1981	President Sadat of Egypt assassinated

Index

About the Contributors

Richard F. Grimmett is a specialist in national defense with the Foreign Affairs and National Defense Division, Congressional Research Service at the Library of Congress. He has written a number of studies dealing with international security affairs and security assistance issues. Grimmett received his Ph.D. from Kent State University where his research centered on congressional and presidential interaction in the development of U.S. foreign and national security policy since world War II.

Franklin D. Kramer is an attorney with Shea and Gardner. He was formerly principal deputy assistant secretary of defense for International Security Affairs during the Carter adminstration.

Robert B. Mahoney, Jr. is a senior analyst at Kaman Tempo. His research interests include the roles played by perceptions in national security decision making, crisis management, and U.S. and foreign nuclear weapons policies. He received his Ph.D. in political science from Northwestern University in 1974.

David L. Wallace is a graduate of the Georgetown University School of Foreign Service. He has worked as a research assistant to James E. Schlesinger, for the Commission on Security and Economic Assistance, and at CSIS.

About the Editors

Lt. Gen. Ernest Graves, USA, retired is Senior Fellow in international security studies with the Georgetown University Center for Strategic and International Studies. He served as CSIS project coordinator for the State Department's Commission on Security and Economic Assistance (Carlucci Commission) in 1983. Graves is a graduate of West Point and holds a Ph.D. from the Massachusetts Institute of Technology. He culminated a thirty-seven-year career as an Army officer with his assignment as director of the Defense Security Assistance Agency from 1978 to 1981.

Steven A. Hildreth is a Fellow in international security studies at the Georgetown University Center for Strategic and International Studies. He has been with CSIS since 1981. From 1979 to 1981 he worked for Senator Frank Church (D-Id.). In 1983 he worked with the CSIS secretariat for the Commission on Security and Economic Assistance. Hildreth has written several articles on international security issues and published *Modern Weapons and Third World Powers* (1984) and *Third World Regional Powers and the Future of Conflict* (in press). He recently served on the Advisory Council of the International Studies Association in the Washington, D.C., region. He received his B.A. from Brigham Young University and his M.A. from Georgetown University.